The Gaslight Effect Recovery Guide

The Gaslight Effect Recovery Guide

Your Personal Journey to Healing from Emotional Abuse

Robin Stern, PhD

RODALE

NEW YORK

Published in the United States by Rodale Books, an imprint of
Random House, a division of Penguin Random House LLC, New York.
RodaleBooks.com
RandomHouseBooks.com

RODALE and the Plant colophon are registered trademarks of
Penguin Random House LLC.

Library of Congress Cataloging-in-Publication Data
Names: Stern, Robin, author.
Title: The gaslight effect recovery guide / Robin Stern.
Description: First Edition. | New York : Rodale, [2023] | Includes bibliographical references and index.
Identifiers: LCCN 2022019719 | ISBN 9780593236277 (trade paperback) |
    ISBN 9780593236284 (ebook)
Subjects: LCSH: Manipulative behavior. | Control (Psychology) | Stress management.
Classification: LCC BF632.5 .S747 2023 | DDC 158.2—dc23/eng/20220914
LC record available at https://lccn.loc.gov/2022019719

ISBN 978-0-593-23627-7
Ebook ISBN 978-0-593-23628-4

Printed in the United States of America

Book design by Andrea Lau
Cover design by Irene Ng

1st Printing

First Edition

For Scott and Melissa,
you are my most special "forever presents."

And for all those who have suffered the soul-destroying effects of gaslighting,
the confusion of losing the ground they walk on, or struggled with tattered self-esteem
because of another. And for all who have taken the journey with me to a gaslight-free life.
You have my deepest gratitude. You are my teachers.

CONTENTS

Preface

The term *gaslighting* is everywhere. We started hearing it in the run-up to the 2016 presidential election as we witnessed with our own eyes events that were later denied. We saw it in social media campaigns that were just not true but that we were expected to believe. Also in 2016, while I wrote the new introduction to *The Gaslight Effect* for the rerelease, the American Dialect Society recognized *gaslight* as the "most useful" new word of 2016. In 2018, *gaslighting* was the runner-up in the Oxford University Press list of the most popular new words of the year. As I am writing this recovery guide in 2022, gaslighting is the topic of at least two television series: *Inventing Anna,* about a socialite grifter; *Gaslit,* about the Watergate scandal; and *Bad Vegan,* a documentary about a top vegan restaurant and what happened to its restaurateur. The Chicks recently released a new album, *Gaslighter,* and singer-songwriter TUCKER's song "Can't Help Myself," released in 2022, was written from the point of view of someone suffering from the Gaslight Effect. (I was honored to join him with a vocal performance about gaslighting, for the song.)

While gaslighting is a relatively new concept for many, I have been exploring this space for three decades. Even before I published the book, I had worked with scores of clients who had experienced gaslighting in their own lives. In 2007, with the first publication of my book, I coined the term *Gaslight Effect* and brought attention to the impact of gaslighting on the lives of people who experienced it. My 2019 article on gaslighting for Vox media is currently one of the top results on Google when people search for the word *gaslighting*. More than one thousand other articles online link to my piece. Since the rerelease of my book, now translated into fifteen languages, I am interviewed frequently by media outlets all over the world.

But, more importantly, I speak to patients weekly and national and international audiences often, and I receive email after email asking for help from people experiencing and suffering from the Gaslight Effect. I am writing this recovery guide for everyone I've talked to, for those who have written to me through the years, and for all those people who have wanted to write but didn't.

The opportunity is now yours—an opportunity for self-discovery, an opportunity for a deeper understanding of gaslighting, and an opportunity for charting your own recovery. I am honored to spend this time with you.

Introduction

Dear Readers, it is my hope that you can use this guide to explore and work through any confusing, difficult, and painful gaslighting relationships to reclaim your sense of self and your reality. You might be feeling annoyed and worried that the outrageous things your gaslighter says could continue. Or, worse, you might be feeling as if your soul is hurting and you are far from the person you were before you met your gaslighter. Perhaps your life has become joyless. No matter where you start, I know you will find solace in understanding how you and your gaslighter are dancing the Gaslight Tango.

At the time I wrote *The Gaslight Effect* in 2007, *gaslighting* was a term I rarely heard in popular discourse, but I saw the tattered lives it produced every day in my therapy practice and even among my friends. I would receive email after email asking for help. "Okay," people have written, "I read your book and I now know that I'm being gaslighted. I know it's destroying my joy and killing my spirit—but why am I doing it and how can I get out?"

I am so pleased to offer you the help and resources in this workbook. The opportunity for self-discovery, establishing a deeper understanding of personal dynamics, and embracing your recovery is now yours. I urge you to engage page by page, step-by-step, one insight and many emotions at a time. Healing from an abusive relationship is no easy task, but it's a necessary one if you want to move forward and reclaim your life.

I am with you every step of the way and will see you through—I believe in your personal power to recover from gaslighting and to move on to nourishing, loving, and respectful relationships where you stand in your integrity. I am cheering you on!

What's Real?

The Gaslight Culture—Gaslighting is insidiously pervasive in today's culture, where people are feeling more anxious than ever. We are inundated by an onslaught of news and information that we're aware might not be accurate, as stories keep changing, often with little or no explanation.

We're surrounded by mixed messaging, which creates both personal and cultural confusion for the individual.

- Though we are well past the Barbie-doll phenomenon, **advertising** still insists that a woman must be a certain size and age to attract a man. Advertisers also tell us that to enjoy life and feel fulfilled we must follow their lead.

- During this time of **social isolation** in a digital and pandemic world, social media comforts our natural desire to connect with others. However, it can leave us wide open to negative social comparisons as well as outright abuse, which could lead to anxiety, an unhealthy outlook toward oneself, eating disorders, and depression. Social media influencers alter their appearance with apps and then deny their usage, causing us to look critically at our own bodies and faces.

- Depending on the point of view of the **media** outlet, simply reporting the facts is becoming increasingly rare. Sowing seeds of confusion, division, and outright hostility seems to be an acceptable trend, as "opinion news" seeks to persuade the viewer that what we saw with our own eyes didn't really happen.

- In the **workplace,** our manager reassures us that we are on track for a promotion but at the same time excludes us from leadership meetings and presents our material as their own. We all know who is doing the hands-on work, but upper management turns a blind eye if the bottom line is met, savings are made, and personal and political alliances maintained.

- **School officials** tell us that we shouldn't pressure our children about grades and instead should focus on what our children are interested in. Yet, everyone knows that grades and test scores determine the student's road forward.

- **Politicians** often give us one reason for their actions, then switch positions for political reasons midstream and offer another, without acknowledging that it's the new "party line." It's all just in a day's work.

In such a climate, we become less certain of what we believe. We are presented with more occasions to question what we know and consequently are more vulnerable to gaslighting than ever. Gaslighting is most painful when it takes place in the privacy of your home but can also be mind-bending when it involves politicians, industry leaders, public figures, and reporters who may all unite to convince us that an incident, which may have been recorded on video, did not occur. It seems lying is now an acceptable option in the public square, with no apparent accountability.

Rather than being encouraged to discover or create our own reality, we are bombarded with powerful demands to ignore our own observations and responses and to accept whatever need or view is currently being marketed.

In that sense, I believe, we are living in a Gaslight Culture, where willful manipulation of another's reality has become common practice and, sadly, our everyday backdrop. Unfortunately, these soul-destroying lies can lead us to be more susceptible to gaslighting in our personal relationships as well.

Unexpected "Wow" Moments

What has *unexpectedly* come to your mind? A place to keep your spontaneous insights... _____

_____

_____

_____

_____

I Offer This Book to You If . . .

You are curious to find out what gaslighting is and whether you are in any gaslighting relationships.

You suspect that you are being emotionally manipulated but can't quite put your finger on it.

You are feeling overwhelmed by the mixed messaging pervasive in our society.

You are looking for solutions to help free yourself from unhealthy or abusive relationships.

You would like to regain your joy, creativity, and powerful sense of self.

You would like a personal experience that expands your awareness and provides solutions.

You would like to identify any potentially unhealthy relationships in your life.

You would like to deepen your self-awareness and become conscious of your habitual feelings and behaviors, some of which may be negative and unproductive.

You are involved in an uncomfortable, destructive, and unhealthy relationship and would like to find out what you can do to change it.

In Your Own Words

What is *your* reason for reading this book? What are you hoping to take away?

I want to…

_____

_____

_____

_____

_____

How to Use This Book

This workbook speaks directly to you, the reader. I hope to provide a meaningful and illuminating experience for you. Think of this book as a personal psychological journey. It's not a psychotherapy session but still a healing process. The relational behaviors and activities in *The Gaslight Effect* have been presented here as an in-depth personal exploration and interactive experience. You will find all the information and context you need to understand and participate in your personal healing process with the full force of your courage, insight, and intention.

There are three different ways you can choose to use this workbook.

A Companion Workbook

You can use this workbook as a companion to *The Gaslight Effect,* moving through the book and the workbook, simultaneously, chapter by chapter. I suggest a slow, steady pace, giving yourself time to savor the unique content in each and reflect and record your thoughts and feelings.

A Unique and Personal Experience

Or, if you prefer, you can simply experience this guide as a unique personal journey, opting to focus entirely on your exploration, personal growth, and relationships. At times this exploration will take you deeply into your own experience and memories. You may find it takes you away from the intellectual exercise of learning about gaslighting for a moment. But don't worry—I'll help you find your way back and further understand how to recognize, avoid, and heal from gaslighting relationships.

Two Unique and Powerful Experiences

Another option would be to first read *The Gaslight Effect* to learn about gaslighting and the insights provided by the different relationships described in the case material. Then take a deep dive into your own personal experience with the workbook, fortified with the knowledge and your feeling-response from the book.

Or you can mix it up however you choose! Whichever way you would like to experience this workbook, you are going to learn more about the insidious and pervasive influence of gaslighting. As you move through the workbook, you will find unexpected insights about yourself and your relationships and will learn what you can do to improve your relational world.

I only ask that you do your best to bring your whole self to the experience and that you be courageous, honest, and compassionate with yourself. Believe me, you are not alone. We all experience challenging and painful moments in our relationships—and we all seek to heal ourselves.

Before we jump in, let's do a quick "Before" exercise, which we will repeat at the end of your journey.

Your Before Responses ...

(Please write your responses to the following comments as if someone had just said this to you.)

1. "You're overreacting, and everybody knows it!"

\
\
\
\
\

2. "You're being irrational . . . again. I'm just telling you this for your own good."

\
\
\
\
\

3. "If you were a considerate partner, you would have made sure you got there before the store closed."

\
\
\
\
\

4. "I never said that to you. You must be starting to lose your memory."

_____

_____

_____

_____

_____

5. "Can't you see how those guys are looking at you? You know you're flirting—just admit it."

_____

_____

_____

_____

_____

What Is Gaslighting?

In this chapter, we'll explore the Gaslight Effect, identifying what it is and the telltale signs that may signal you are involved in a gaslighting relationship. To provide context, we'll dig deeper into the progressive stages of gaslighting and the three most common types of gaslighters. I encourage you to bring your intelligence, intuition, sensitivity, and insight to this unique and personal journey.

What Is Gaslighting?

Gaslighting is an insidious and sometimes covert form of emotional abuse, repeated over time, where the abuser leads the target to question their judgments, reality, and, in extreme cases, their own sanity.

Gaslighting is a type of psychological manipulation in which a gaslighter—the more powerful person in a relationship—tries to convince you that you're misremembering, misunderstanding, or misinterpreting your own behavior or motivations, thus creating doubt in your mind that leaves you vulnerable and confused.

Understanding the Gaslight Effect

The Gaslight Effect results from a relationship between two people: A **gaslighter,** who needs to be right to preserve their own sense of self and to keep a sense of power in the world; and a **gaslightee,** who is manipulated into allowing the gaslighter to define their sense of reality because they idealize the gaslighter and seek their approval. You feel yourself slipping into confusion and self-doubt—but why? What has made you suddenly question yourself? How is it that a person who supposedly cares for you has left you feeling so awful?

Gaslighting is insidious. The gaslighter understands that there are few things as destabilizing as being made to question your own grip on reality. Gaslighting can warp your mind and leave a more powerful impact than physical abuse. It plays on your worst fears, your most anxious thoughts, and your deepest wishes to be understood, appreciated, and loved. When someone you have chosen to trust, respect, or love speaks with certainty—especially if there is a grain of truth in it—it can be extremely difficult not to believe them.

1. **Neither of you may be aware of what's happening.** The gaslighter may genuinely believe that they are saving you from yourself. Remember, they are driven by their own needs to seem like a strong, powerful person, although they may appear to be an insistent, tantrum-throwing child. They know no other way to gain power or to feel secure. They must prove they are right, and you must agree. If even a small part of you feels the need for your gaslighter's love or approval to be whole, you are susceptible to gaslighting. **Gaslighting is always the creation and interplay of two people.**

2. **A gaslighter sows confusion and doubt.**
   - They manipulate someone into questioning their own reality.
   - They don't take responsibility for their actions and try to undermine the credibility of anyone who questions their actions.
   - They attempt to control the gaslightee by questioning their reality and insisting the gaslightee agrees with them.
   - To support their own needs, they undermine someone's sense of self by questioning their reality, belittling their judgments, and redefining who they are.

- They destabilize their partner when they are feeling vulnerable in an effort to feel more powerful.
- They use an implicit threat of abandonment to keep their partner connected by asserting that the gaslightee needs them to define their reality.

3. **A gaslightee is manipulated into doubting their own perceptions to keep the relationship going.**
   - You are manipulated into letting the other define your sense of reality and who you are.
   - When the aggressor asserts their point of view while negating your own, you go along to keep things calm.
   - You support the other's reality at the expense of your own, in the hope of gaining their approval or avoiding unpleasant behavior.
   - You second-guess yourself instead of running the risk of alienating your partner—you leave yourself rather than risk your partner leaving you.
   - You forfeit your personal power and can't find the energy or the will to stand up for yourself in the face of adversity.
   - You need to believe the gaslighter to keep participating in the relationship.

4. **How do you know if it's gaslighting?**
   You may be thinking, "That happens all the time. I always disagree with my partner!" So, what's the difference between gaslighting and . . .
   - Disagreeing with someone?
     - ✔ Discussing and listening to opposing points of view in a respectful manner is a healthy form of debate. It keeps your mind active and helps you form a stronger bond of mutual respect and define boundaries.
   - Trying to influence someone?
     - ✔ There are always times when we attempt to persuade others to agree with us or to go along with our desired plan. Which restaurant should we go to for dinner? Where should we go for vacation? However, this is not a malicious attempt to manipulate the other person into questioning either their grasp on reality or the validity of their personal preferences.
   - Narcissism?
     - ✔ Healthy narcissism can reflect a cohesive sense of self, but unhealthy

narcissism is typically a result of psychological injuries during childhood, leading to adult behaviors that can contribute to total self-involvement and insensitivity to the needs of others. Not all narcissists are gaslighters.

- Bullying?
  - ✔ Bullying is a repetitive behavior (somewhat redefined by the internet) that often includes an imbalance of power and an intent to harm the other physically, mentally, or emotionally. It may include gaslighting but doesn't necessarily involve an intentional undermining of someone's reality—although repeated aggressive criticism may result in the target questioning themself.

- Manipulating?
  - ✔ Manipulation is about intention and degree. Manipulating a situation to achieve a generally positive outcome is different from intentional manipulation that undermines the other's integrity, perception, or self-esteem. When this is done to gain power for personal satisfaction and momentary stability, this is abusive gaslighting.

Are You Being Gaslighted?

Let's Get Personal—Turn up your gaslight radar and check for these twenty telltale signs. Gaslighting may not involve all of these experiences or feelings, but if you recognize yourself in any of them, give it extra attention. *(Check the signs that feel familiar.)*

- ☐ You are constantly second-guessing yourself. You ask yourself, "Am I too sensitive?" a dozen times a day.
- ☐ You often feel confused and even crazy at work.
- ☐ You're always apologizing to your mother, father, partner, or boss.
- ☐ You frequently wonder if you are "good enough."
- ☐ You can't understand why, with so many apparently good things in your life, you aren't happier.
- ☐ You buy clothes for yourself, furnishings for your apartment, or other personal purchases with your partner in mind, thinking about what they would like instead of what would make you feel great.
- ☐ You frequently make excuses for your partner's behavior to friends and family.

- ☐ You find yourself withholding information from friends and family so you don't have to explain or make excuses.
- ☐ You know something is terribly wrong, but you can never quite express what it is, even to yourself.
- ☐ You start lying to avoid the put-downs and reality twists.
- ☐ You have trouble making simple decisions.
- ☐ You think twice before bringing up seemingly innocent topics of conversation.
- ☐ Before your partner comes home, you run through a checklist in your head to anticipate anything you might have done wrong that day.
- ☐ You have the sense that you used to be a very different person—more confident, more fun loving, and more relaxed.
- ☐ You feel as though you can't do anything right.
- ☐ Your kids begin trying to protect you from your partner.
- ☐ You find yourself furious with people you've always gotten along with before.
- ☐ You feel hopeless and joyless.

While all these symptoms can occur with anxiety disorders, depression, or low self-esteem, the difference with gaslighting is that *there is another person or group that's actively engaged in trying to make you second-guess what you know is true.* If you don't typically experience these feelings with other people but do with one particular individual, then you might be a victim of gaslighting.

Telltale Sign—In Your Own Words . . .

Reflecting on personal experience, thoughts, feelings, and behaviors, I realize I often experience or feel . . .

_____

_____

_____

_____

_____

THE THREE STAGES OF GASLIGHTING: FROM BAD TO WORSE

Gaslighting tends to work in stages. At first, it may be relatively minor—indeed, you may not even notice it. Eventually, though, gaslighting becomes a bigger part of your life, preoccupying your thoughts and overwhelming your feelings. Finally, you're mired in full-scale depression, unable even to remember the person you once were. You've lost touch with your own point of view and your sense of self. Of course, you may not proceed through all three stages. But for many who are susceptible, gaslighting goes from bad to worse.

Stage 1: Disbelief

You can't believe your partner is saying such silly things or trying to tell you there's something wrong with you or your actions. Eventually, as your partner continues to insist on their reality and undermine yours, you begin to question if they might possibly be right.

Stage 2: Defense

You are constantly defending yourself and ruminating over what you and your partner said to each other. Who is right? Who is wrong? You can't stand the idea that you might have to walk away—even from an argument—without their approval.

Stage 3: Depression

When you've been gaslighted for a long period of time, you are no longer the same person as when you entered the relationship. You are more isolated, you are often depressed, and you avoid talking about your relationship with others. With your gaslighter, you do your best to avoid anything that might trigger abuse. In this stage, you often take on the gaslighter's distorted and critical judgment of you.

———

Gaslighting may remain at Stage 1 or Stage 2 or go back and forth between them—and that's painful enough. When gaslighting proceeds to Stage 3, however, the results can be truly devastating. Worst of all, you've lost your joy. All that matters to you is getting your gaslighter to love you, to stay with you, and to approve of you.

THREE TYPES OF GASLIGHTERS

1. The Glamour Gaslighter: When They Create a Special World for You

Example—Suppose your boyfriend hasn't called you for two weeks, even though you've left him several messages. Then, when he shows up, he's carrying a huge bouquet of your favorite flowers, a bottle of expensive champagne, and tickets for a weekend getaway. You're angry and frustrated. Where has he been? But he refuses to accept that there was anything wrong with his unexplained absence and insists you join him in enjoying this romantic occasion he's just created.

Like all gaslighters, he's distorting reality and demanding that you agree with his distorted view. He's behaving as though he's done nothing out of the ordinary, acting as though you're the unreasonable one for being upset. Glamour and romance may cover up his behavior and your initial reaction to it.

Are you involved with a Glamour Gaslighter? See if the items on this checklist ring any bells. Although some of the items are negative, many are neutral or positive. But if you are concerned that your partner is using glamour to distract you from your feelings, even the positive items may indicate gaslighting. *(Check items that feel familiar.)*

- [ ] Do you often feel as though the two of you have your own special world?
- [ ] Would you describe your partner as "the most romantic person I've ever known"?
- [ ] Are your fights and disagreements typically followed by intense times of closeness or romance, including special presents, greater intimacy, and better sex?
- [ ] Are your friends impressed by how romantic your partner is?
- [ ] Are your friends nervous about how romantic your partner is?

☐ Does your impression of your partner not match your friends' impression?

☐ Does your partner behave markedly differently in public than in private? Are they the kind of person who needs to charm everyone in the room?

☐ Do you sometimes feel that your partner has a whole repertoire of romantic ideas that don't necessarily fit your moods, tastes, or history together?

☐ Does your partner insist on being romantic—sexually or otherwise—when you've said you aren't in the mood?

☐ Do you feel a marked discrepancy between your experience early in the relationship and your sense of it now?

Dynamics

Undermining a partner's emotions and feelings is a way to deny their reality. Continuous invalidation of how the other person feels about a situation is just as effective as saying their perceptions are wrong. The emotional chopping away during those moments has the effect of convincing you that you could be imagining or "making up" scenarios that don't exist, when in reality, what you are feeling or experiencing is real.

Maybe your partner will make statements such as the ones listed here. Instead of calling them out or silently disagreeing, you buy into their view because you so desperately want to be "one of the family" and your agreement seems to be the price of admission.

✔ You're so sensitive!

✔ You know that's just because you are so insecure.

✔ Stop acting crazy. You sound crazy. You know that, don't you?

✔ There you go getting defensive again.

✔ You just love trying to throw me off track.

✔ I was just joking!

✔ You are making that up.

✔ It's no big deal.

✔ You're overreacting and imagining things.

✔ You are always so dramatic.

✔ That never happened.

✔ You know you don't remember things clearly.

Telltale Sign—In Your Own Words...

I realize that I often lose my courage and can't respond to certain comments like...

_____

_____

_____

_____

_____

UNDERSTANDING THE BEHAVIOR

How Relationships Work: Mirroring and the Developmental Process

There are deeper psychological reasons why so many smart, strong, and independent people can fall prey to gaslighting: (1) The need for the other's **approval** and **to be positively mirrored** is a powerful force we are all susceptible to. (2) Adult **relational dynamics** are largely influenced by the relational milieu we grew up in, which imprints the unconscious belief that what we observed and experienced as a child is how the world and relationships work.

These two environmental influences that shape our early childhood can significantly contribute to or help protect us against getting mired in the gaslighting dynamic. Understanding these elements can help both the gaslightee and the gaslighter learn how to consciously change their relational dynamic.

We will refer to and deepen these concepts throughout the workbook, in addition to learning about Attachment Theory, an important development in psychoanalytic thought.

Let's take a quick dive into the psychoanalytic theory of these basic human developmental needs. My goal is to help you understand the concepts so you can participate more consciously in exploring a process that is key to your emotional healing.

Taking It Deeper—The "Why"

Developmentally, the type of mirroring a child receives from others, positive or negative, contributes significantly to how the child sees themself, thus impacting the child's developing sense of self and personal agency. Mirroring informs how the child unconsciously projects themself. Think of this process as the *lens through which the child habitually views themself and their world,* including *how they engage in relationships.*

This early developmental process sets a child up to believe what they are told about themself, which unconsciously integrates into their developing sense of self. This can manifest as persistent inner-self dialogue or "self-talk," which the child carries into adulthood.

Another key developmental process to consider is how a child learns about relationships (i.e., how they work and how to be in one). This is learned by observing the relationships unfolding around them as well as through direct one-on-one experiences with others. These early relational experiences become what psychologists refer to as "relational schemas" that unconsciously continue to manifest positively or negatively in our adult relationships.

Finding Yourself—Take a Deeper Dive . . .

Listen for the voices of your childhood. Voices that told you things about yourself. Listen for the voices of your parents, older siblings, and friends. Voices that told you who you were, what you were feeling or perceiving. Were they predominantly positive messages or negative messages? Were they pleasant or unpleasant messages? Do you remember what they said? How much of their voice is **your** voice now?

_____

_____

_____

_____

_____

Let's Make It Personal

What were you told about yourself?

_____

_____

Do you remember who told you? Did you believe it?

_____

_____

Does any of it surprise you? As you remember, how do you feel?

_____

_____

What thoughts accompany your feelings?

_____

_____

Have you incorporated any of their talk about you into your talk about you?

_____

_____

2. The Good-Guy Gaslighter: When You Can't Quite Say What's Wrong

Example—Paula said she respected Sandi and consistently told Sandi that she really wanted to please her. But most of the time, no matter the content of the conversation, whenever Sandi offered an alternate view, Paula suggested that maybe Sandi was overanalyzing again or that maybe she was overly sensitive and worrying—as usual—too much. Paula had a lovely manner and an agreeable personality, and she would completely undermine Sandi, with a smile and by using the mildest tone. In the end, that disregard and disrespect were all Sandi took away from the discussion—and the back and forth left her frustrated and exhausted, whether she "won" or "lost."

If you're involved with someone like this, you may often feel confused. You may feel dismissed or disrespected—that your wishes and concerns never really get through—but you can never quite put your finger on what happened or what's wrong. After all, your partner is "so nice"!

Are You Involved with a Good-Guy Gaslighter?

(Check the signs that feel familiar.)

- ☐ Is your partner constantly working at pleasing you and other people?
- ☐ Does your partner offer help, support, or compromises that somehow leave you feeling frustrated or vaguely dissatisfied?
- ☐ Is your partner willing to negotiate household, social, or work arrangements with you, but you still never quite feel as if you were heard, even though you've presumably gotten what you asked for?
- ☐ Do you feel as though your partner always gets their way, but you can never quite figure out how that happened?
- ☐ Do you feel as though you never quite get what you want, but you can't quite put your finger on what you have to complain about?
- ☐ Would you describe yourself as perfectly happy in your relationship but somehow feeling numb, disinterested, or discouraged about life in general?
- ☐ Does your partner ask you about your day, listen attentively, and respond sympathetically, yet somehow, you end such conversations feeling worse than before?

Telltale Sign—In Your Own Words . . .

(If you think you may be involved with a Good-Guy Gaslighter . . .)

The relationship just feels "off," but I'm not sure why. I think I'm feeling . . .

_____

_____

_____

_____

They seem like a really good person because . . . but at times they . . .

_____

_____

_____

_____

The last time I felt genuinely joyful in the relationship was . . .

_____

_____

_____

Dynamics

Gaslighting is the undermining of your sense of reality by a gaslighter who needs to be right, regardless of their personality type. What you take away from the conversation is not what actually happened, but the covert message, "You're wrong, and I'm right!" Here, the gaslighter is caught up in the need to bolster themself and tenaciously holds on to the certainty of their "rightness." For example, the Good-Guy Gaslighter needs to do nice things to prove what a good person they are—even as, or just after, they dismiss or discount what you think. Not surprising that you often feel lonely, even if you don't know why.

UNDERSTANDING THE BEHAVIOR

Sense of Self: The Ideal Self and the Actual Self

We all have a sense of self—an idea of who we are, a perception of our many attributes and traits that characterize us—including our personality, our likes and dislikes, our strengths and weaknesses, our unique perspective, our identity, our behavior. The sense of self has two major components: the **Ideal Self** and the **Actual Self.**

The Ideal Self—This is the self that we desire to be, aspire to be, and work toward. We usually want to project our Ideal Self to others in the hope that we will be positively "met," acknowledged, respected, and even admired and loved. Early parental mirroring plays a key role in the development of the Ideal Self. Think of it as the child learning what they "should be." (Note: It is important that this early mirroring be realistic and factually based, reflecting the child's natural talents and abilities. Absent this mirroring, the child can develop an unhealthy grandiosity, believing they possess exaggerated talents and abilities, or a deep-seated sense of inadequacy, for not living up to the Ideal Self projected onto them by the parent.)

The Actual Self—This is the self that constitutes who we believe we are right now in time. The Actual Self is made up of feelings, thoughts, attitudes, and behaviors in the here and now, especially feelings about ourselves. This is also called the **Self-State,** which can fluctuate from moment to moment. For example, one moment we might be feeling self-confident, strong, in control, and even superior. But the next moment we might feel fearful, weak, scared, anxious, depressed, inadequate, unsure, shameful, or guilty. These represent the **vulnerable feelings** of the Actual Self. While we all experience these feelings, we generally don't like them. Thus, our natural reaction is to view them as negative aspects of who we are. Our own discomfort with these feelings leads us to try to keep them hidden from others and even from ourselves. In this way, the vulnerable feelings of the Actual Self can become the enemy of our Ideal Self. The best outcome is to be conscious of the vulnerable feelings we are suppressing and use that energy to understand, work through, and embrace our whole and real self.

- The vulnerable feelings aspect of the Actual Self is similar in origin for the gaslighter and gaslightee. However, despite having similar origins, it manifests very differently.

- For the gaslighter, we see narcissistic grandiosity; for the gaslightee, we see a lack of personal agency. In either instance, the behavioral manifestation represents a defense against feared or believed inadequacies.

Taking It Deeper—The "Why"

Ideal Self versus Actual Self in the Gaslighter and Gaslightee

The Gaslighter cannot tolerate any challenge to their Ideal Self, to their ideas or perspectives, and especially to their competence. They cannot tolerate vulnerable feelings in themself or others.

In contrast, the Gaslightee can be plagued with vulnerable feelings, especially feelings of inadequacy.

Both the Gaslighter and Gaslightee can go to extreme lengths to keep their vulnerable feelings hidden, including developing personality disorders, anxieties, depression, and addictions.

GASLIGHTER

Ideal Self—Typically, the Ideal Self is dominant for the Gaslighter, which they believe totally defines their sense of self. Any challenge to the Ideal Self can quickly result in a fierce response or reaction and a fragmented self-state (i.e., a lack of self-cohesion and personal agency).

Actual Self/Vulnerable Feelings—The Gaslighter is terrified of being wrong or seen as weak, inadequate, and ineffectual.

GASLIGHTEE

Ideal Self—Typically, the Gaslightee does not lead with their Ideal Self by presenting a "low profile." This is because they have learned not to trust themself and to accommodate and acquiesce to others. Specifically, the Gaslightee does not trust the validity of their needs, wants, or perspectives (i.e., habitually believing their needs, feelings, and perspectives should come second to others).

Actual Self/Vulnerable Feelings—The Gaslightee fears rejection and abandonment. They work hard to be accepted by readily forfeiting their needs, wants, and perspective. In extreme cases they will fully accept their vulnerable feelings as totally defining their sense of self.

Note: Self-state is a term used to describe your emotional and psychological equilibrium in the moment, which can fluctuate between positive or negative. The term refers to the degree of **self-cohesion** (how much a person trusts themselves, the degree of equilibrium, and sense of personal agency) a person feels in the moment. A lack of self-cohesion, or a **fragmented** self-state, typically produces feelings of anxiety, frustration, annoyance, mistrust, and irritability.

Finding Yourself—Take a Deeper Dive . . .

Reflect on your Ideal Self, the person you work hard to be and to present to the world. The Ideal Self you hope everyone sees and respects. *The person you believe you should be.*

Describe your Ideal Self. Include in that description, the "you" you want to be.

I am . . . _____

I'm not . . . _____

I desire to be . . . _____

Now reflect on your *Actual Self,* especially your feelings about yourself.

I am . . . _____

I need . . . _____

I want . . . _____

Is there a part of you that's hiding? Can you coax this part of you to come out into the open? What are the more persistent vulnerable feelings of your Actual Self? Are they hard or easy for you to touch?

_____

_____

_____

Can you feel a change in your self-state when you get in touch with these feelings?

_____

_____

Remember to have compassion for *all* of you—even the parts that are hard to face and the emotions that are scary to feel.

Remember, you may not know all your answers yet. Be gentle with yourself and have patience.

"Barriers to My Actual Self"

What barriers may get in the way of being your Actual Self and exposing your vulnerable feelings?

_____

_____

_____

_____

_____

3. The Intimidator Gaslighter: When He Bullies, Guilt-Trips, and Withholds

Example—Glamour gaslighting and Good-Guy gaslighting are often hard to spot because so much of their behavior is desirable in other circumstances. But some gaslighting behavior is more obviously problematic: yelling, put-downs, freeze-outs, guilt trips, and other types of punishment or intimidation.

In some cases, these problematic actions alternate with Glamour or Good-Guy behavior. In other cases, they characterize so much of the relationship that it would be correct to call your gaslighter an Intimidator.

Are You Involved with an Intimidator?

(Check the signs that feel familiar.)

- ☐ Does your partner put you down or find other ways of treating you with contempt, either in front of other people or when the two of you are alone?
- ☐ Does your partner use silence as a weapon against you, either to get their way or to punish you when you displease them?
- ☐ Does your partner frequently or periodically explode into anger?
- ☐ Do you find yourself feeling fearful in their presence or at the thought of them?
- ☐ Do you feel that your partner mocks you, either openly or under the guise of "just kidding" or "just teasing"?
- ☐ Does your partner frequently or periodically threaten to leave if you displease them, or do they suggest or imply that they may leave?
- ☐ Does your partner frequently or periodically evoke your worst fears about yourself? For example: *"Here you go again—you're so demanding!"* or *"That's it—you're just like your mother!"*

Telltale Sign—In Your Own Words . . .

Do you feel worn down or depleted by surprise attacks and have no desire or energy to defend yourself? Most of the time I'm really feeling . . .

_____

_____

_____

_____

_____

_____

Dynamics

Being involved with an Intimidator can be doubly challenging. To make your relationship more satisfying, both of you will need to work on two areas: the gaslighting and the intimidation. The latter is particularly unpleasant and scary, even when it's not part of gaslighting. Ultimately, if you choose to work on the relationship, the Intimidator in your life will need to alter their way of relating to you and learn more skillful and healthier ways of communicating as you work on tolerating discomfort by either walking away or setting boundaries if they continue to be aggressive. That said, let me say again that you should never have to tolerate physical or emotional abuse.

*Chaos contains information that
can lead to knowledge—even wisdom.*

—Toni Morrison

UNDERSTANDING THE BEHAVIOR

Healthy Narcissism versus Unhealthy Narcissism

The greater a person's confidence about how they see the world, the more comfortable they will be holding onto their own perceptions and reality, regardless of how many people challenge their grasp of the facts. But the unhealthy narcissist who is rigidly certain about their perception may easily become enraged when others don't share their views.

For the person struggling with unhealthy narcissism, disagreeing with them can represent a challenge to their sense of superiority.

The Intimidator is dependent on feeling superior. They fear the loss of control over how others see them and cannot tolerate having their Ideal Self questioned or undermined.

In this example, it is easy for narcissism to have a bad name. We all need some healthy narcissism, but it is important to understand the underlying vulnerability.

Taking It Deeper—The "Why"

Narcissism has a bad reputation. But is it really *all* bad?

We all need what psychologists refer to as healthy narcissism: that is, a strong sense of self—knowing what you need and want and appreciating who you are.

Unhealthy narcissism often results from an emotionally difficult and potentially traumatic childhood (lack of warmth, neglect, or excessive praise), resulting in a fragile sense of self. To compensate for this fragile self, the child develops a stance that looks like self-centeredness. Developmentally, this fragility can also result in a worldview that others are not to be trusted and relationships will always be painful. This worldview can lead to the deep belief that it is safer to only project one's Ideal Self while remaining as distant as possible from others but while pretending to be emotionally connected. Such a worldview means it is essential to stay in control of projecting one's Ideal Self and personal perspective.

In contrast, healthy narcissism helps us maintain our personal viewpoint and boundaries and makes it possible for us to be more empathic with others.

Finding Yourself—Take a Deeper Dive ...

What do you believe you need to be your strong self?

What do you believe is essential to maintaining your well-being, balance, and purpose in the world? How might you put that need into words?

I need… _____

I want… _____

I believe that I deserve to have… _____

_____

How does it feel to acknowledge your own need?

_____

_____

How easy or hard was it to describe what you deserve?

_____

_____

Are you surprised by any of your answers?

_____

_____

How do you feel if someone questions you and your need?

_____

_____

How do you respond inwardly and react outwardly?

_____

_____

As you experience your feelings, do you also feel any resistance or barriers to those feelings?

_____

_____

Now, give yourself permission to appreciate yourself in words.

_____

_____

River Story

Visualization

For a few minutes, allow me to guide you in taking a deep dive into the river of your life, looking for touchstones in the water . . . those defining moments when your own reality-perception-feelings were encouraged—or when they were squashed.

This inner journey can enhance your insight about your vulnerability to gaslighting.

Part 1: Close Up

- Write the date of your birth in the bottom-left corner of a blank page and today's date in the upper-right corner.
- Next, draw the "river of your life" between the date of your birth and today's date. It can be a straight line, have many twists and turns, tributaries, or no tributaries—it's your decision.
- Now, close your eyes (if comfortable) or simply gaze gently downward. Imagine that you are on the bank of the river and getting into a personal hovercraft that will float two feet above the water. You will travel in this hovercraft following the river of your life from the date of birth to the present date.
- As you float along, notice the touchstones beneath the water and allow them to represent those defining moments when your own perceptions or feelings were either encouraged or squashed. Note those defining moments emblazoned in your memory.
- Write or draw those defining moments in your river and take a few minutes to "be" in the moment and notice details—Where are you? What is around you? Who is with you?—and emotion nuances—What do you feel? What comes to your mind? An example:

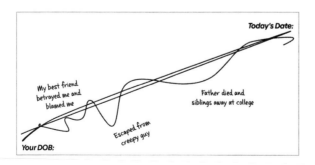

Try not to make any judgments about your observations and insights. Be curious instead.

The important thing is for you to get to know and understand yourself, and moments that have shaped you, more intimately and lovingly.

Defining Moments

Now, write or draw these defining moments that are emblazoned in your memory.

What do you notice?

Any surprises?

Are your defining moments usually with people or when you are alone?

Are your defining moments mostly pleasant or unpleasant memories?

Today's Date:

Your DOB:

Ripples of Memory

Part 2: The Big Picture

- Now imagine that you left your hovercraft by the riverbank and now you are in your own hot air balloon floating high above the river, so you have a higher and broader perspective.
- As you move along between the defining moments of your life, looking down at the river of your life between the date of your birth and today's date, allow yourself to notice those moments when your perceptions or feelings were either encouraged or squashed, now from a new perspective way up high.
- Identify one or two of those moments that stand out for you right now.
- Please circle those moments. Now, spend a few minutes writing about these moments.
- Does anything surprise you as you look at the moments you identified? Where were you—describe it in detail. What happened? Who was there? What did you feel? What was the immediate impact in your life at the time? What was the long-term impact of this moment? Do you still feel its impact today? What are you thinking and feeling now that you have explored those memories?

Unexpected "Wow" Moments

What has *unexpectedly* come to your mind? A place to keep your spontaneous insights . . . _____

_____

_____

_____

2

The Gaslight Tango

In this chapter, we will take a closer look at the Gaslight Tango and the ways our own behavior, desires, and fantasies may be leading us into the dance. Fortunately, there is a solution to the problem of gaslighting. When you realize that you alone can define your sense of self—that you are a worthy person who deserves to be loved, regardless of what your gaslighter thinks—you've taken the first step toward freedom. You have found a deep source of power within yourself that will help free you from the Gaslight Effect. The first step is to become aware of your own role in gaslighting.

Example—Sarah knows there is something radically wrong with the way her boyfriend talks to her. She used to just say, "He's a jerk" in her head and wonder why she stayed with him. He has been demeaning and insulting for months now, telling her that she must be dreaming if she thinks her work is valued or that coworkers really count on her input. He always has an awful sneer on his face when he tells her about her incompetence and blindness to it. He is so convinced! She thinks he is wrong but still wonders: Does he have a point? She hates the way he sees her and is good at defending herself and her work, but it's getting exhausting. She can't stand that he thinks so little of her.

People who become victims of gaslighting are often terrified of being misunderstood or can't stand being miscast. Despite the confidence and strength they frequently display, in reality, they are extremely vulnerable to the opinions of their loved ones and associates.

Remember, gaslighting is a way to control the moment in a relationship, to stop the conflict, to ease anxiety, and to feel "in charge" again. It's a cognitive strategy to help the gaslighter self-regulate and try to coregulate. Your gaslighter may not even know they are doing anything manipulative, and they may just think they are expressing themself directly or just prone to unflinching honesty. When this honesty includes your gaslighter telling you who you are, and how you think and feel, it will drive you crazy. When you are trying to defend yourself, dancing the Gaslight Tango, you do not have the ability to step back and be objective about your gaslighter's motivation. You simply feel the onslaught of another person's beliefs about your thoughts and behaviors, which can feel judgmental, controlling, and infuriating.

In intimate relationships, both people are often vulnerable to the other and tend to give away a lot of power to the person they love. In this setup, being misunderstood can feel like a death blow or an invitation for battle.

1. Dancing the Gaslight Tango

Although gaslighting looks like the work of a single, abusive gaslighter from the outside, **a gaslighting relationship always involves the active participation of two people.** You can end the gaslighting as soon as you stop trying to win the argument, convince your gaslighter to be reasonable, or prove that you are right. **Instead, you can simply opt out—** that is, step out of the tango and take your power back, while resisting the pull to try to change your gaslighter's perceptions.

Let's take a closer look at the intricate steps of the **Gaslight Tango**.

Step 1. The dance usually begins when a gaslighter insists that something is true despite your "deep knowing" that it is false. For example: *"You know you are so forgetful; you know that you are!"*

Step 2. Gaslighting can occur only when a gaslightee tries—consciously or not—to accommodate the gaslighter, or to get them to see things the gaslightee's way, because they seek approval. For example: *"I am not forgetful! I never miss an appointment! How can you say that? I have never even been late."*

Step 3. Rather than stick with their own perceptions, when a gaslightee is worn down, they try to win the gaslighter's approval by finding a way that the two of them can agree and be joined in their reality. They pivot. Most often, they pivot by giving in and accepting the other's reality at the expense of their own.

Making It Personal—In Your Own Words...

Gaslighting is not your fault. Sometimes you don't know you're stepping into it, but when you do realize what's happening, you can use your power to **pivot out** and say you just don't want to do it anymore.

Can you think of a time you felt wrongly accused? When you were told you were doing something wrong or misperceiving something? Your gaslighter was likely persistent and accusing, and then you pivoted in their direction, agreeing with them.

_____

_____

_____

_____

Can you remember the pivot and why? What were you thinking?

_____

_____

_____

_____

What emotions did you allow yourself to feel?

_____

_____

_____

_____

_The last of human freedoms—the ability to choose
one's attitude in a given set of circumstances._

—Viktor E. Frankl

2. Why Do We Go Along with It?

1. Fear of the Emotional Apocalypse
2. The Urge to Merge

Fear of the Emotional Apocalypse

First, let's look at the Emotional Apocalypse. The Emotional Apocalypse is an explosion that flattens everything in its vicinity and poisons the atmosphere for weeks afterward. A person in a gaslighting relationship fears that if the gaslighter is pushed too far, they will evoke the Emotional Apocalypse. This apocalypse is such a painful experience that eventually you will do anything to avoid it.

If you never know when your partner might explode in rage, after a while you may find yourself giving in to whatever they said, just to keep the yelling at bay.

The Emotional Apocalypse can take many forms depending on your circumstances. For example, it can come from a boss who threatens professional defeat or a family member who paralyzes you with guilt.

The worst effects of gaslighting are the loss of confidence, loss of joy, disorientation, deepening depression, and allowing the gaslighter to define your worldview and sense of self. Giving in completely—in thought, emotion, and action—may come to seem like the only safe course.

Apocalypse Now: The Gaslighter's Secret Weapon

What do you find most painful? Your gaslighter is an expert at using your vulnerability as their secret weapon. *(Check the signs that feel familiar.)*

They may . . .

- ☐ Remind you of your worst fears: "You really are too fat/frigid/sensitive/difficult . . ."
- ☐ Threaten you with total abandonment: "No one will ever love you again." "You'll be single for the rest of your life." "No one else would put up with you."
- ☐ Evoke other troubled relationships: "No wonder you can't get along with

your parents." "Maybe this is why your friend Suzi dropped you." "Don't you see this is why your boss doesn't respect you."

- [ ] Use your ideals against you: "Isn't marriage about unconditional love?" "I thought friends were supposed to be supportive." "A true professional would be able to take the heat."
- [ ] Make you doubt your own perceptions, memory, or sense of reality: "I never said that—you only imagined it." "You promised to take care of that bill; don't you remember?" "My mother was really hurt by what you said." "Our guests thought you were ridiculous—everyone was laughing at you."

Reflection—Let's Get Specific

Can you reflect on a time when you felt the emotional devastation of accusations like the ones mentioned here, or any other kind of emotional threat? It may be painful to recall these experiences. If it is, reframe the moment by reminding yourself that you are on the road to healing . . . to uncovering . . . to taking your power back. I am asking you to please trust the process and yourself.

_____

_____

_____

Can you reflect on a time when you were feeling good (happy, accomplished, or safe) and then felt the devastation of an emotional threat?

_____

_____

_____

> Can you remember a time when you shared something positive and your partner threw it back in your face as a negative?
>
> _____
>
> _____
>
> _____

Before moving on, please take a moment to breathe and release any feelings this exercise may have triggered for you. Believing your gaslighter's accusations and your response is *not* the truth about yourself, but your worst apocalyptic fears that threaten your sense of self.

Remember: You are a good and worthy person who deserves to be loved, regardless of what your gaslighter thinks.

The Urge to Merge

The Urge to Merge is the second reason we give up our own perceptions to join in the Gaslight Tango. No matter how strong, smart, or competent we are, we feel an urgent need to win the approval of the gaslighter, whom we've idealized and allowed ourselves to need. If both partners are doing well, they may allow each other more room. If one or both are feeling vulnerable, they may require greater "loyalty"—that is, unconditional agreement—from each other.

When a gaslightee feels anxious about disagreement or disapproval, they tend to respond in one of three ways.

1. They quickly **align themself with their partner.**
2. They try to **induce their gaslighter—through argument and/or emotional manipulation—**to come around to their own point of view so they can feel secure and valued.
3. They **pivot to avoid the apocalypse,** after their partner's insistence and their own protesting wears them down.

In each response, the gaslightee is willing to do almost anything to protect their sense of being close to their gaslighter, even if it means annihilating their own sense of self in the process.

Making It Personal—In Your Own Words

Do any of these responses feel familiar to you? If so, which one or ones?

_____

_____

_____

UNDERSTANDING THE BEHAVIOR

Urge to Merge: Similarity of the "Why" in Gaslightee and Gaslighter

The Urge to Merge describes the unconscious phenomenon where the gaslightee gives up their sense of self to maintain a positive connection with the gaslighter.

But **why**? This relational dynamic is part of the **Gaslight Tango** where each person unconsciously steps into their choreographed parts of the dance.

Taking It Deeper—The "Why"

For the Gaslightee, the Urge to Merge is an attempt to maintain a positive connection by providing positive mirroring and empathy for the gaslighter. The unconscious strategy here is to avoid demonstrating a disappointment in the gaslighter and bringing on a possible confrontation—the Emotional Apocalypse! The goal is to maintain a positive relational connection at all costs. This "at all costs" behavior by the gaslightee can indicate a fragile and insecure sense of self and a form of *pathological accommodation.* Typically, this relational strategy was learned in early childhood to maintain a positive attachment and connection with one or both parents and to ward off abandonment anxiety.

The gaslighter's part in the dance also indicates a fragile sense of self but one that manifests very differently. While the gaslightee compensates by giving up their sense of self, the gaslighter compensates by *demanding that the other conform to their perspective or reality and positively mirror their Ideal Self.* In so doing, the gaslighter *mistakes the gaslightee's agreement and capitulation* for genuine empathy and positive regard. Nonetheless, the gaslighter uses this to shore up their fragile sense of self.

Finding Yourself—Take a Deeper Dive...

Describe your fragile feeling self.

_____

_____

_____

Does that part of yourself feel familiar?

_____

_____

_____

Are you comfortable in exploring it further? **Y / N** (If "No," please just jump ahead to where you are comfortable.)

_____

_____

If "Yes," please use the space here to note where your fragile feeling self shows up.

_____

_____

_____

How do you protect this vulnerable part of yourself?

_____

_____

_____

What are your thoughts and feelings about this part of yourself?

_____

_____

_____

Your Part in the Tango

It takes two to tango: Are you becoming a gaslightee? See what you learn by taking the following quiz. Be as honest as you can.

Scenario 1: Mother—Your mother has been calling for weeks to try to get you to make a lunch date, but you've been swamped. Between your new boyfriend, your recent bout with the flu, and your mounting deadlines at work, you just can't find the time. She says, "Well, I can see that you don't care about me at all. It's nice to know I raised such a selfish daughter!"

You respond:

a. ___ "How can you say I'm selfish? Can't you see how hard I'm working?"

b. ___ "Gosh, I'm so sorry. You're right. I'm a terrible daughter. I feel awful."

c. ___ "Mom, I have a hard time talking to you when I feel like you're putting me down."

Scenario 2: Friend—Your best friend has just canceled on you at the last minute, yet again. You gather your courage and say to her, "It really drives me crazy when you cancel on me like that. I end up alone on a weekend night, feeling lonely and abandoned. I'm frustrated because I could have made plans with somebody else. And frankly, I miss you!"

In a warm, concerned tone, your friend says, "Well, I've been meaning to tell you, I think you're becoming a little too dependent on me. I'm a little uncomfortable spending time with someone who is so needy."

You respond:

a. ＿＿ "I'm not needy. How can you say I'm needy? I do things by myself all the time! I just don't like it when you cancel on me—that's the problem!"

b. ＿＿ "Wow, is that why we don't spend time together? I guess I'd better work on that. I'm so sorry to be a burden."

c. ＿＿ "I'll think about that. But how did we get from you canceling on me at the last minute to me being needy?"

Scenario 3: Supervisor—Your supervisor has been under a lot of pressure lately, and you think she's taking it out on you. Although there are times when she praises you to the skies, there are other days when you walk into her office and she reads you the riot act for minor infractions. She's just spent ten minutes pointing out that your choice of typeface on your latest market analysis has violated the company's standard format. "Why do you insist on making my job so difficult?" she asks. "Do you think you deserve special treatment? Or do you have some kind of problem with authority?"

You respond:

a. ＿＿ "Oh, get over yourself—it's only the typeface!"

b. ＿＿ "I don't know what's wrong with me lately. Maybe I do have some issues to work on."

c. ＿＿ "I'm sorry I didn't follow procedure." (Thinking: "I really hate being yelled at.")

Scenario 4: Boyfriend/Girlfriend—Your boyfriend/girlfriend has been moody and withdrawn all evening. Finally, they blurt out, "I don't see why you have to tell my secrets to the whole world." As you prod them for details, the story emerges: You told someone at his/her office party about the Caribbean vacation that the two of you are planning. "It's nobody's business where we go!" they insist. "People get all sorts of clues from information like that—how much money I'm making, how my sales have been going—things I don't want them to know. I told you that. Obviously, you have no regard for my privacy or respect for what I ask."

You respond:

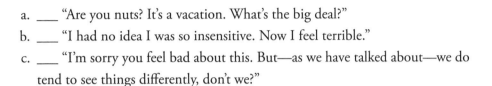

a. ___ "Are you nuts? It's a vacation. What's the big deal?"
b. ___ "I had no idea I was so insensitive. Now I feel terrible."
c. ___ "I'm sorry you feel bad about this. But—as we have talked about—we do tend to see things differently, don't we?"

Scenario 5: Spouse—You and your spouse have been locked in the same conversation for hours. You've failed to get to the dry cleaners, as you had agreed to do, and now your spouse doesn't have the coat they intended to take on a business trip the next day. You apologize but insist it wasn't intentional—you simply got to the cleaner's five minutes after it closed. They point out that you're always late when it comes to doing them favors; this isn't the first time you've screwed up. You agree that you are chronically late but insist that it's not directed against them personally. Your spouse accuses you of trying to sabotage the trip so they'll have to stay home with you. Or maybe you're jealous of their new coworker. Or maybe you're just tired of your own job and envious of how much they like their job.

You respond:

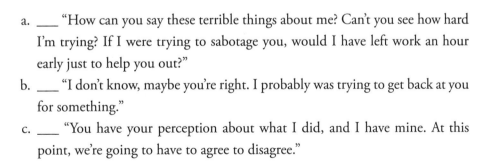

a. ___ "How can you say these terrible things about me? Can't you see how hard I'm trying? If I were trying to sabotage you, would I have left work an hour early just to help you out?"
b. ___ "I don't know, maybe you're right. I probably was trying to get back at you for something."
c. ___ "You have your perception about what I did, and I have mine. At this point, we're going to have to agree to disagree."

Answer Key

If you answered "a" to most of these scenarios: You're locked into an ongoing argument with your gaslighter—an argument you can never really win. By needing to win your gaslighter's approval, you give them the power to "make you crazy." Even if you're right, you might consider ways to opt out of the arguing so you can end the dance.

If you answered "b" to most of these scenarios: Sounds like your gaslighter has already convinced you to see things their way. Because you want their approval so much, you're willing to agree with them—even at the expense of your own self-esteem. But even if you've made a mistake, you don't need to agree to your gaslighter's negative view of you.

If you answered "c" to most of these scenarios: Congratulations! Every one of these answers is a terrific way to step gracefully out of the Gaslight Tango. Because you're more committed to your own sense of reality than to winning your gaslighter's approval, you have the power to opt out of arguments and interrupt the gaslighting. You're well on your way to freeing yourself from the Gaslight Effect.

Reflection—How Did You Do?

Where did most of your responses fall?

a. Locked into wanting the other's approval.
b. Accepting the other's reality at the expense of your own.
c. Opting out of the tango.

Using a scenario of your own—something that has happened recently or something from a while ago that you wished you had handled differently—how would you change your response to step more clearly away from the tango?

_____

_____

_____

_____

What do you imagine would have been the consequence (short term or long term) between you if your words had the impact you desired?

_____

_____

_____

Remember: As long as there's any part of yourself that believes you need your gaslighter—to feel better about yourself, to boost your confidence, or to bolster your sense of who you are in the world—you'll be leaving yourself open for gaslighting.

> *Between stimulus and response there is a space.*
> *In that space is our power to choose our response.*
> *In our response lies our growth and our freedom.*
>
> —Viktor E. Frankl

The Empathy Trap

Now, let's look at one more aspect of the Gaslight Tango that can lure us into that dangerous dance: the **Empathy Trap**.

Empathy is the ability to imagine what another person is feeling by putting yourself in his or her place. You share in their fear, hurt feelings, and frustrations by connecting to the way you felt when you were afraid, frustrated, or disappointed. And when you hear that your friend's health is fine, that your child has a new friend, or that your partner just got a promotion, you participate in their joy as well.

Empathy is the balm that makes sorrow bearable and the gift that multiplies joy, helping us to feel less alone and reassuring us that we are loved and understood.

But empathy can be a trap, and never more so than in a gaslighting relationship. Your very ability to offer empathy—and your own need to receive it—opens your personal boundaries and can make you prone to the Gaslight Effect if you don't know how to protect yourself.

You can get stuck in someone else's shoes and take on their feelings as if they were your own, losing sight of your own feelings and personal boundaries.

Example—Katie's empathy made it hard for her to choose her own worldview over that of her boyfriend. She was so compelled to see things from Brian's point of view that she was willing to let go of her own perspective.

Most of the time, Brian was aware only of his own needs and feelings. Acknowledging that she might feel differently than he did was like admitting that his feelings were invalid. Katie wanted to see her boyfriend's point of view, but he didn't want to see hers.

Empathizing with Brian made Katie feel sensitive and loving. But when Brian was asked to empathize with Katie, he felt weak and defeated. Katie's overzealous empathy led her to disregard her own feelings and perceptions. Her need for Brian's empathy and approval was so great that it threatened to overwhelm her ability to think clearly. This desperate need for approval, understanding, and love kept Katie continually open to Brian's gaslighting. Falling into the Empathy Trap and seeing and feeling the world according to Brian made it hard for her to step back into her own shoes. Trapped in her own empathy, she would often excuse his behavior, which kept her from reframing her situation and on the slippery slope to accepting gaslighting.

UNDERSTANDING THE BEHAVIOR

Avoid the Empathy Trap and Free Yourself

The Empathy Trap results from the gaslightee's Urge to Merge, along with their instinct to offer empathy to the gaslighter to maintain a positive relational dynamic. The gaslightee has learned to use empathy and positive mirroring as a manipulation tool for relational survival, which paradoxically becomes a trap.

When you have to give up your own perspective to offer empathy, it is not true empathy. **True empathy does *not* require you to give up your perspective.** In fact, you cannot be truly empathic with another if you do not know what you are feeling in the moment. So, it is important to recognize and to clarify that your own thoughts and feelings are legitimate and that you cannot be manipulated into giving them up.

Taking It Deeper—The "Why"

The "As-If" Stance—Resisting the Urge to Merge and Avoiding the Empathy Trap

The "as-if" stance is a psychological process where we maintain awareness of our own feelings and perspective while attempting to tune in and understand the *what* and *why* of the other's feelings and inner experience.

This is especially difficult to do when being told by the gaslighter that your feelings or perspective are wrong and illegitimate. This demand by the gaslighter sets up the Empathy Trap.

The Empathy Trap can be avoided and eliminated by cultivating awareness of your own feelings, trusting their validity, and then attempting to connect with the other person's feelings **as if** they were your own. This requires giving yourself permission to feel and maintaining healthy boundaries—that is, not confusing the other's feelings with your own. In a healthy relationship, this is a reciprocal process.

Finding Yourself—Take a Deeper Dive . . . Where Do Your Feelings End?

Are you able to tell the difference between your feelings and the feelings of the person you are talking to?

_____

_____

Have you ever noticed that you have suddenly taken on the feelings of another person?

_____

_____

In trying to understand how the other person is feeling, have you ever lost sight of what you were feeling?

_____

_____

Have there been times when you might be projecting your feelings onto the other person?

_____

_____

Making It Personal—Try completing the following sentences about a relationship that you find troubling, sticking entirely to your own point of view. I suggest writing down your answers, speaking them aloud, or both. You may find it helpful to hear and see your own perspective, not just think it!

In this relationship, I feel _____

_____

Something I would like to change is _____

_____

I can't stand it when _____

_____

_____

I see myself as basically _____

_____

_____

I like it when people _____

_____

_____

How did it feel to complete those sentences? If you found yourself having a hard time, feeling uncomfortable, or even panicking, don't worry. That's just evidence of how new it is for you to focus so completely on your own perspective. Try sitting with the feelings and seeing what emerges.

You might also find it easier to think of these big questions in more simple, concrete ways.

This week, one thing I would like my partner to do is _____

_____

_____

Tomorrow, one thing I wish could be different would be _____

_____

_____

One thing I like about myself is _____

_____

_____

Start with Recognizing Your Feelings—Many people are not aware of how they really feel nor do they give themselves permission to allow and explore emotions. This may have to do with childhood conditioning. For example, you may have been taught that your feelings weren't important. Maybe you were told, "I don't care what you are feeling—go to your room" or "You don't hate your brother—you love your brother." Maybe the importance and validity of feelings were not positively modeled. If your family didn't talk about emotions or ask you about your feelings, you were given the message that emotions were not to be talked about or were too private or scary to be shared.

With compassion for our parents and relatives who likely did not have an emotional education, it is not hard to understand why many of us are not practiced in knowing and managing our emotions. But researchers in emotion science tell us that when you can name your feelings, you can begin to manage them. When you can't name your feelings, you may learn, for example, to "calm down" by taking a few deep breaths when you feel big feelings. But calming down doesn't fully address disappointment, envy, or many other emotions.

Whatever the initial cause, *the result is that we often avoid, suppress, or judge our true feelings; confuse feelings like anger and disappointment; or judge hurt as weakness.*

It is important to find clarity about what you are really feeling and why. Once you are aware of your feelings, you can begin to embrace those that are productive and life affirming and shift away from those that are unproductive and destructive.

Here, with a long list of emotions and with a tool for building self-awareness, you can begin to build your emotion vocabulary and awareness of the complexity and dynamics of feelings.

Know Your Emotions

> *When we don't have the words for our feelings,*
> *we are not just lacking descriptive flourish.*
> *We are lacking authorship of our own lives.*
>
> —Dr. Marc Brackett, founding director, Yale Center for
> Emotional Intelligence and author of *Permission to Feel*

Build a "Feelings Vocabulary"—Gaslighting often leads you to ignore, disavow, re-press, judge, or even to lose touch with, your feelings. And, when you don't know how you feel, you're out of touch with a key source of information about yourself. Giving yourself permission to feel is the first step. Next is to name and understand your feelings, which can help you effectively deal with them and stand up to your gaslighter.

It is so important to name the particular emotion you are experiencing. A nuanced feelings vocabulary can help you build a mental model of your emotions. Then, when you're ready to tell your gaslighter how you feel and what you want, you'll have the words right there.

Science says there is a difference between emotions and feelings. Emotions are an immediate, unexpected response to something that has happened inside or outside of you that causes a shift in your physiology and thinking, body language, facial expressions, and vocal tones.

Feelings are your private psychological experience of what's going on inside or outside of you.

But for our purposes in this book and ease of reading, I will use feelings and emotions inter-changeably as a single, combined experience and response.

Consider the words in the following list and circle those feelings that are familiar to you.

Abandoned	Ecstatic	Insecure	Satisfied
Adequate	Embarrassed	Intimidated	Shocked
Affectionate	Energetic	Isolated	Shy
Ambivalent	Excited	Jealous	Silly
Anxious	Exhausted	Judgmental	Sluggish
Appreciated	Exhilarated	Lonely	Stunned
Bad	Fearful	Lovable	Threatened
Bored	Frantic	Loving	Thwarted
Comfortable	Frustrated	Miserable	Tired
Confident	Glad	Misunderstood	Touched
Creative	Good	Needy	Troubled
Curious	Grateful	Nervous	Uncertain
Defeated	Guilty	Optimistic	Uneasy
Dejected	Happy	Outraged	Uptight
Dependent	Hostile	Overwhelmed	Violent
Depressed	Inadequate	Paranoid	Vulnerable
Desperate	Incompetent	Pleasant	Wonderful
Determined	Independent	Preoccupied	Worried
Disappointed	Infatuated	Rejected	
Discontented	Inferior	Relieved	

Can you add more words that describe how you feel?

_____	_____	_____	_____
_____	_____	_____	_____
_____	_____	_____	_____
_____	_____	_____	_____
_____	_____	_____	_____

ACCESS YOUR IDEAL ADVISER

Visualization

Visualize a wise person whom you trust entirely. You can visualize a real human being, a magical or spiritual guide, or even an animal. Picture this guide witnessing a recent troubling incident with your gaslighter. He or she sees everything that happens with perfect clarity. Imagine going to visit this guide after the incident. What does your guide say to you about what happened?

_____

_____

_____

_____

_____

_____

Talk to Someone You Trust

- If you've got a friend or relative whom you really trust, explain that you're doing an exercise in discovering or rediscovering your own point of view.
- Try telling this person exactly what you think about a troubling or confusing situation that involves your gaslighter.
- Ask the person to interrupt you gently—perhaps simply by holding up a hand or using a signaling word whenever they hear you slipping out of your own point of view and into anyone else's, especially your gaslighter's.

The goal is for you to clarify your own thoughts and feelings, without reference to anyone else. Make sure this person doesn't insert their own opinion!

Reflection

After you have been able to connect with your friend or relative, reflect on your feelings about the experience and answer the following questions as honestly as possible.

Do you remember when they signaled you to stop? Did you understand why they interrupted you at that moment?

_____

_____

_____

Did you agree with them?

_____

_____

_____

How did you feel when they interrupted you?

_____

_____

_____

What was your response?

_____

_____

_____

Was the exercise helpful to you? If yes, why? If no, why not?

_____

_____

_____

The World Is Your Laboratory—If you want to know what your friend or relative thinks (most of us do), make a date to discuss this exercise in a day or so. Then try living for twenty-four hours with only your own opinion in your head.

Unexpected "Wow" Moments

A place to keep your spontaneous insights . . . _____

_____

_____

_____

_____

Keep away from people who try to belittle your ambitions.
Small people always do that, but the really great
make you feel that you, too, can become great.

—Mark Twain

3

Stage 1:
"What Are You Talking About?"

In the next three chapters, we'll look at some specific ways you can identify and free your-self from the gaslighting dynamic as you move through the three stages of gaslighting: from the seemingly trivial to the overwhelming.

Entering Stage 1: A Crucial Turning Point

The tricky thing about Stage 1 gaslighting is that it seems so minor. Just a little misunder-standing, just a moment of discomfort, just a tiny loss of temper or a petty disagreement. But these seemingly trivial events can be the warning signs that herald a destructive pattern and often prove to be a crucial turning point in a relationship.

Example—John was stuck waiting for the bus. He knew he would be a few minutes late to meet Brandy, his girlfriend, for lunch. He tried to call her, but she didn't pick up. When he got to the coffeeshop she wasn't there. He checked his messages but didn't have any from her. He waited half an hour and called her again—no answer. He didn't mind waiting, but he was a little worried and more than a little annoyed. She was late all the time. He really liked her and hoped that it would mean something to her that he waited every time she was late. John opened his computer and started working.

Brandy got there just shy of an hour late and breezed in with a warm hello. John said,

"So happy to see you! I was worried when you were late." Her expression turned sour and she replied contemptuously, "Late—c'mon, here we go again. You can't keep your schedule straight and, as usual, you want me to take the rap for your flakiness."

"What?" he thought to himself. Then, aloud, he said with certainty, "No, my scheduling is fine, thank you. I won't make a big deal, but you were fifty-five minutes late, and it's not the first time. An apology would be nice."

A clear, decisive refusal of Stage 1 gaslighting may enable you to nip those tendencies in the bud and go on to a gaslight-free relationship. Just like John did in the example here, in this chapter, I will show you exactly how to opt out of Stage 1 gaslighting.

Sometimes gaslighting will begin in a relationship that has felt relatively healthy for weeks, months, or even years. Your mutual history may make it that much harder to realize that your spouse, friend, or boss is gaslighting you.

The sooner you recognize any gaslighting tendencies and stop playing into the pattern, the better chance you have of restoring your previously gaslight-free relationship, and the choice to go or stay will be less painful. If you have a gaslighting relationship with someone you can't avoid (a boss, relative, or colleague) you can limit your contact with the person and cut back on your emotional involvement.

Identifying the dynamic will help you be aware of your own tendencies to dance the **Gaslight Tango** and begin rewriting your own gaslight-prone responses, while the gaslighting is still manageable and your sense of self is relatively intact.

Stage 1 Gaslighting: Telltale Signs

If you feel anxious, sad, or a sense of recognition as you read through these lists, or if any of the signs ring a loud bell, pay attention. Your internal response may be your way of letting yourself know that you've entered the first stage of gaslighting.

Signs That You Have Entered Stage 1
(Check the signs that feel familiar for each relational context.)

With a Lover or Spouse

☐ You often argue about who's right and who's wrong.

☐ You find yourself thinking less about what you like and more about if they are right.

☐ You can't understand why they so frequently seem to be judging you.

☐ You often have the sense that they are distorting reality, remembering or describing things differently from the truth. The way they see things often makes no sense to you.

☐ Your perception of the relationship is that it's going well, except for these isolated incidents that keep sticking out in your mind. When you describe your partner's point of view, your friends look at you like you're crazy. When you try to describe what's bothering you about the relationship to others or yourself, you find yourself unable to convey the problem.

☐ You don't tell your friends about those small incidents that disturb you; you'd rather just ignore them.

☐ You actively cultivate friends who think you're in a good relationship.

☐ You think of your partner as masterful and in charge rather than controlling.

☐ You think of your partner as glamorous and romantic rather than unreliable and unpredictable.

☐ You think of your partner as reasonable and helpful—then wonder why you don't feel better about the relationship.

☐ You feel protected and safe with your partner and unwilling to give up that safety just because of some occasional bad behavior. When they're possessive, moody, or preoccupied, you see how troubled they are and want to make things better.

☐ You call them out on their behavior, and it goes nowhere. But you keep hoping it will.

With a Supervisor or Boss

☐ Your boss tells you about yourself all the time, and most of it is negative.

☐ Your boss praises you to your face, but you have the feeling that they're undermining you behind your back.

☐ You feel there's nothing you can do to please your boss.

☐ You used to feel competent at work and now you don't.

☐ You're always checking out perceptions with your coworkers. After you leave work, you're constantly replaying conversations you had with your boss. But when you replay those conversations, you can't quite figure out who's right, and you can't quite remember what they said—but you know you felt attacked.

With a Friend

- ☐ You frequently disagree. Every disagreement seems to become personal, even if nothing is actually said about you.
- ☐ You often don't like the way your friend appears to regard you and are frequently trying to change their opinion.
- ☐ You avoid certain topics of conversation.
- ☐ You feel put down by your friend.
- ☐ You find yourself not wanting to make plans with this friend.

With Family

- ☐ Your parents' or relatives' perception of you doesn't match your perception of yourself, and they're happy to tell you about it.
- ☐ Your siblings are constantly accusing you of behaviors or attitudes that you don't believe you have.
- ☐ Your siblings have an image of you and of themselves that you just don't see, and they insist that you share it.
- ☐ Your siblings insist on treating you as though you were stuck in your childhood role. If you're the youngest, they treat you as if you were still acting like a baby. If you're the oldest, they behave as though you were still bossing them around.
- ☐ You're frequently defending yourself.
- ☐ You feel like you're never doing enough.
- ☐ You feel like a bad kid for asking for something.
- ☐ You find yourself feeling guilty more often than not.

Reflection—Rate Your Relationships

After checking off the signs that feel familiar in the relationship samples on the previous pages, consider how you would **rate the number of signs** you checked for each category. On a scale of 1 (rarely), 2 (sometimes), and 3 (often), rate your relationships by the frequency of gaslighting behaviors you experience in your own life.

Remember that a single gaslighting interaction doesn't mean it's a gaslighting relationship, but recognizing those moments allows you to prevent Stage 1 from progressing any further.

Lover or Spouse

- ☐ 1 (rarely)
- ☐ 2 (sometimes)
- ☐ 3 (often)

Supervisor or Boss

- ☐ 1 (rarely)
- ☐ 2 (sometimes)
- ☐ 3 (often)

Friend

- ☐ 1 (rarely)
- ☐ 2 (sometimes)
- ☐ 3 (often)

Family

- ☐ 1 (rarely)
- ☐ 2 (sometimes)
- ☐ 3 (often)

Were there any surprises as you completed this checklist?

_____

_____

If so, write a bit about what you became aware of. Allow your memories and feelings, without judgment. Most of us have experienced some form of gaslighting at some point in our lives. Take a moment and notice what feelings are coming up for you right now.

I am feeling: _____

_____

_____

_____

You can reference your "Feelings Vocabulary" list (page 43).

> *Sometimes carrying on, just carrying on,*
> *is the superhuman achievement.*
>
> —Albert Camus

Who's Crazy: Me or Them?

It's always important to allow your feelings and to unpack the information they offer. Once you stop ignoring them and permit yourself to get in touch with your emotions, you can determine the most productive way forward.

Sometimes your discomfort is a signal to be cautious and sometimes it's a warning signal that indicates danger—and you'd be foolish to ignore it. So, my advice is to find your **Flight Attendants**, some trustworthy indicator—*other people, gut feelings,* or *your inner voice*—to help you sort out when your anxiety is warranted and when it's just a feeling that you may want to put on hold.

Flight Attendants

Flight Attendants Who Might Signal Danger

____ Frequent feelings of being bewildered or confused

____ Bad or restless dreams

____ A troubling inability to remember details of what happened with your gaslighter

____ Physical indicators: sinking stomach, tight chest, sore throat, intestinal difficulties

____ A sense of dread or hyper-alertness

____ An extra effort to convince yourself or your friends of how good the relationship with your gaslighter really is

____ The feeling you're tolerating treatment that compromises your integrity

____ Trusted friends or relatives who frequently express concern

____ Avoidance of your friends or refusal to talk with them about your relationship

____ A loss of joy in your life

Stage 1 gaslighting is insidious. It may not involve any of the signs we traditionally associate with emotional abuse—no insults, cutting remarks, put-downs, or controlling behavior. But gaslighting, even in this early phase, is profoundly destabilizing and undermining. You may have that vague sense that something is wrong, something you can't quite put your finger on.

You have two choices when confronted with a gaslighter's negative response: to remain gaslight-free or to remain gaslight-prone.

Making It Personal—In Your own Words

Who are *your* Flight Attendants, and how do they warn you?

_____

_____

Can you think of a time you relied on your Flight Attendants to get you out of a psychologically dangerous situation?

_____

_____

Choice #1: Gaslight-Free

- **Partner**—You are strong and centered, uninterested in your date's approval and grounded in your own reality. You see their annoyance as a reflection of their own anxieties. You understand their childhood injuries that you want to help heal. But you know it's their problem, not yours. You've refused the opportunity to be gaslighted.

- **Work**—You are relatively confident about yourself and your work. What your boss thinks about you doesn't really penetrate deep into your sense of who you are. With that self-esteem, you may be able to shrug off the odd interpretation and avoid gaslighting.

- **Family**—If you have a good sense of yourself as a kind, loving, and generous person, your relative's distortions of reality won't bother you too much. You may even view them with compassion, reminding yourself that they're probably nervous about the party as you shrug off their inaccurate account of your actions.

Choice #2: Gaslight-Prone

- **Partner**—You're likely to strive for their approval and fear that if this wonderful person thinks you're too sensitive, maybe you are and maybe that's the problem. The way to win their approval is to agree with their perception. And so the Gaslight Tango begins.

- **Work**—If your sense of self depends on your boss's approval, you might start to wonder if maybe they have a point. As soon as you begin giving space to their theories, knowing they are not true, you've opened yourself to further gaslighting.

- **Family**—If you are invested in your family thinking well of you, your relative's distortions might throw you for a loop. Maybe it's true—maybe you are a bad, selfish person who neglects your family. So, you desperately try to convince them of your good intensions.

UNDERSTANDING THE BEHAVIOR

Our Vulnerable Feeling Self and the Need to Maintain a Positive Connection

It's psychologically dangerous when our entire sense of self depends upon our partner's approval and view of us! However, it is a human need to be positively regarded and accurately mirrored by the people we have chosen to love and to trust.

When we permit ourselves to need the other (especially in a vulnerable way), we are particularly susceptible to their negative mirroring (for example, *"You never/always/persistently—get it/do it/see it wrong"*). We begin to believe these condemnations about who we are and how we are perceived in the world.

The emotional manipulation implicit in negative mirroring undermines our self-confidence and personal agency. We can end up feeling unlovable, which can reinforce our worst fears about ourselves. It makes sense that these moments would be very painful!

Taking It Deeper—The "Why"

Our Vulnerable Feeling Self

Exposing our vulnerable feeling self to those we have chosen to "need" can be a scary proposition—especially when we are feeling our most fragile.

When our childhood parental-mirroring is mostly negative, critical, and judgmental, we are likely to develop an insecure, fragmentation-prone sense of self with real or feared inadequacies, guilt, and shame. This is our vulnerable feeling self. Our inner dialogue revolves around the question, "How can I get them to see me, approve of me, and love me?"

It can be devastating when our gaslighter's judgments and condemnations replicate our childhood injury and poke at our vulnerable feeling self.

Finding Yourself—Take a Deeper Dive...

Does any of this feel familiar? Would you like to take a closer look?

_____

_____

What has come to mind for you as you read through this?

_____

_____

Would you say you were generally positively or negatively mirrored as a child?

_____

_____

How has the negative and critical mirroring played out in your relationships?

_____

_____

How has the positive and supportive mirroring played out in your relationships?

_____

_____

I invite you to take a moment to give yourself compassion and encouragement—whatever words you want to say to give yourself a verbal hug. This work is challenging. And be sure to celebrate your courage as you keep moving forward.

I can be someone's and still be my own.

—Shel Silverstein

Stage 1 Gaslighting Occurs More Easily . . .

(Check the items that feel familiar to you.)

- ☐ If you are easily swayed by people who seem certain.
- ☐ If you are responsive to people who seem hurt, frustrated, or needy.
- ☐ If you have a strong need to be right and to be seen as right.
- ☐ If you have a big stake in being liked, appreciated, or understood.
- ☐ If it's important to you to be able to fix things and make everything come out well.
- ☐ If you have a huge capacity to feel for others and find that you can shift all too quickly to your gaslighter's point of view.
- ☐ When you want very much to preserve the relationship.
- ☐ If you want to keep relationships going—you have a hard time letting go of people.
- ☐ When you want to preserve your good opinion of the gaslighter.
- ☐ If you have a hard time acknowledging that someone is treating you badly.
- ☐ If you feel very uncomfortable with disagreement or conflict.
- ☐ If you are more comfortable relying upon another person's opinion rather than your own.
- ☐ If you worry frequently about not being good enough, capable enough, or lovable enough.
- ☐ If you want to win your gaslighter's approval, especially because you have idealized or romanticized them, or because you're invested in preserving the relationship.

Telltale Sign—In Your Own Words . . .

Are you concerned with any of the items you checked?

_____

_____

Do any of them feel more concerning than others?

_____

_____

_____

Which one would you most like to change?

_____

_____

Would it be possible? How would you go about doing it?

_____

_____

_____

When Criticism Becomes a Weapon

Suppose you're involved with a man who occasionally loses his temper and yells. You hate being yelled at, but you're willing to tolerate it. When your guy bursts forth in a loud voice, you say calmly, "Please don't yell at me. Let's put this whole argument on hold and just go to bed." But he continues, saying, "I don't see why you have to be so sensitive!" or "I wasn't yelling; I was speaking in a normal voice."

Again, you have choices for how to respond. For example, you could say, "I don't want to continue this conversation" or "I guess we see things differently" or even "You *might* be right" (without saying that he *is* right). You may still be able to end the argument with your sense of self intact. But if you can respond without capitulating to his point of view, your choice is a refusal of the Urge to Merge, which is great self-protection.

Learning to see yourself through a loved one's eyes can be a tremendous catalyst to growth, just as being receptive to criticism is part of any important relationship.

However, sometimes *a gaslighter will use criticism as a weapon that makes you feel overly anxious, hurt, and vulnerable*. That criticism becomes their Emotional Apocalypse. Because you're so vulnerable to it, you will begin to do anything to avoid it. The criticism may be partly true, but its intention is to undermine, not to help.

The minute you sense that you're being undermined or attacked, you should stop listening to the words and focus on how you feel, which is the main point: You don't deserve to be treated that way, no matter what you have or haven't done.

Criticism That Is Intended to Undermine Often …

1. Includes name-calling, exaggeration, or insults.
2. Comes during a fight or an angry exchange.
3. Is presented as part of a person's efforts to win an argument.
4. Is made over your objections or your wish to end the conversation.
5. Seems to come out of nowhere.
6. Changes the focus from the other person's behavior to yours.
7. Is given in a context where you cannot easily respond.

This point is so important, I'm going to repeat it.

You should never listen to criticism that is primarily intended to wound, even if it contains a grain of truth, or more than a grain of truth. *If your Flight Attendants tell you that someone is using truth as a weapon, stop listening and remove yourself from the conversation* or you risk being drawn into the Gaslight Tango.

Your legs will get heavy and tired. Then comes a moment of feeling the wings you've grown, lifting.

—Rumi

The Explanation Trap

This is **an effort to explain away behavior that disturbs you,** including gaslighting. You find seemingly rational explanations to prove to yourself why these danger signals aren't really dangerous.

You're trying to pick and choose, deciding which part of a gaslighter's behavior to respond to and which part to ignore. Try to slow down your responses and be aware of your own behavior, feelings, and motivation. Ask yourself if you are caught in the **Explanation Trap**.

Here are four ways you might imprison yourself in the Explanation Trap.

1. **"It's Not Him, It's Me"**—We interpret everything that happens in the relationship as our own doing. It's a sneaky way of saying that we're all-powerful. If our gaslighter's bad behavior is all our fault, then we've got complete control of the situation. Or sometimes, it is too scary to see the gaslighter as responsible. Once we see it, we have to make hard choices.

2. **"He Feels So Bad"**—We confuse the other person's sorrow, anger, or frustration with genuine regret. By focusing on his bad feelings, we deceive ourselves into believing that he really does care for you. Through the power of fantasy, we see, not a self-absorbed man who was barely aware of our feelings, but a sensitive, caring guy who was upset about what he had done.

3. **"No Matter How She Behaves, I Should Rise Above It"**—We can always try to convince ourselves that we are, or should be, unaffected by another person's bad behavior. Sometimes we simply "decide" not to mind a certain action; we basically forget it happened. Either way, we're trying to make ourselves seem so strong that the gaslighter's behavior cannot affect us.

4. **"Unconditional Love"**—You can insult me, ignore me, or make unreasonable demands, and I won't be affected in the least. That's how good a person I am and how much I love you. In the end, you and your behavior don't really matter; all that matters is that "we love each other."

UNDERSTANDING THE BEHAVIOR

Explanation Trap and the Mutual Impact Dynamic—What each partner does affects the other—it is love's sorrow and its joy. It's not possible to remain unaffected by the other person's behavior; if we could, we would just have the entire relationship by ourselves. We may come to feel, consciously or unconsciously, that love really isn't an option, that we'll never meet anyone who's capable of giving to us generously, caring for us with empathy, and supporting us the way we need and want. We may try to solve the problem all on our own by re-creating ourselves as strong, self-sufficient, and all-powerful. This can have the effect of denying the other's agency and diminishing the relationship's potential for joy.

Instead of looking at how we feel in a relationship—satisfied or empty, loved or neglected—we cling to a fantasy and **try to short-circuit our loved one's shortcomings by explaining them away or trying to become better people ourselves.** We deny and enable their gaslighting and manipulative behavior toward us. We develop an extraordinary tolerance for psychological mistreatment and drama, all in the interest of holding onto the fantasy and the relationship. And so we leave ourselves wide open to gaslighting.

I'm all for people sticking out the bad times in a relationship. I believe that any loving relationship requires a certain amount of self-sacrifice—love isn't always easy. My goal is to help you become aware of any potentially damaging patterns and behaviors in your relationship and to help you work through them in the most constructive way possible.

Check In with Your Reality: Remember What Goes on During Gaslighting— Even if your gaslighter is capable of genuinely relating to you some of the time, they can become overwhelmed by their own need to restore their sense of self and sense of power by proving to you that they are right and insisting that you agree. No matter how much they talk about you and your feelings, they are really concerned with only one thing—getting you to agree they are right. This can be especially true if the gaslighter has had a bad day where they can't control their environment, for instance, at work or with their social group.

Taking It Deeper—The "Why"

The Mutual Impact Dynamic refers to how two people react and respond to each other in the moment. It can be positive, negative, or neutral. Relationships are a dynamic system, meaning how we impact each other is in a constant state of potential change.

It is also important to recognize that each person has some choice in how they react and respond in the moment. For example, what we say and do, and how we say it (or don't), has a huge impact on how the other reacts and responds. In this way, each person shares some of the responsibility for the co-created relational dynamic.

If you are focused on controlling the relational dynamic and denying bad behavior, either yours or your partner's, you are living a lie for both people.

Finding Yourself—Take a Deeper Dive…

As you begin to explore your childhood beliefs about yourself and how relationships work, I invite you to reflect on those that impact your tendency to ignore or explain away either your behavior or your gaslighter's.

What do you believe about relationships in general that may be contributing to your explaining away your gaslighter's behavior? *For example: "I believe that no one can give me what I really need."*

_____

_____

_____

Can you remember when you began to believe this?

_____

_____

How has this belief contributed to the choices you have made in this relationship?

_____

_____

_____

How have your choices impacted the other person and your relational dynamic overall?

_____

_____

_____

You may try to find some way to explain their behavior, crafting a reassuring explanation that makes you entirely responsible for everything that goes wrong and so, presumably, entirely capable of fixing it.

Consider that, in your own way, you may be disregarding your partner's needs as much as they are ignoring yours. *(That doesn't mean gaslighting is acceptable, but it may help you consciously act to change the relationship for the better.)*

Making It Personal—In Your Own Words . . .

Do you think your partner has needs you may have been disregarding?

_____

_____

_____

I realize now that my partner needs _____ from me that I haven't been aware of.

What has blocked my willingness to see this? *For example: "In the moment I am so defensive, I can only defend myself."*

_____

_____

_____

Why haven't I responded to those needs? *For example: "In the moment I am so angry at his gaslighting response, I ignore them and reject him."*

_____

_____

_____

While struggling with the Gaslight Effect, it may be difficult to reflect on your role in the tango. Please remember to check in with your feelings and have patience and compassion for yourself.

How Can You Escape the Explanation Trap?

Stay in touch with your Flight Attendants (page 52). They will help you see the difference between explanations that genuinely illuminate a situation and those that help you ignore reality.

If you're feeling anxious, unsettled, or disturbed and have to keep repeating your explanation over and over again—to yourself or to a friend—that's a pretty good sign you're trying to explain something away. *A genuine explanation brings the relief of understanding and compassion. An Explanation Trap often feeds the very anxieties it's meant to diminish.*

Some Ways to Access Your Flight Attendants—As you work on these activities, feelings may come up that make you uncomfortable. That is okay—in fact, it's a sign that you're accessing the very internal wisdom you need to solve the problem. Just hang in there, observe the feelings, and see what they have to teach you.

- **Keep a journal.** If you are feeling troubled or uncertain, commit to filling at least three pages daily for at least seven days. Write as quickly as you can, without pausing to censor yourself or consider your thoughts. Allow your truth to emerge.

- **Give yourself the permission to feel all your feelings.** Remember that all feelings are okay and give you information. Your emotional life can give you answers to simple questions: Does that situation or person leave me feeling uplifted and pleasant or unpleasant and unhappy? Greet each feeling with curiosity—what is your emotion telling you?

- **Meditate.** Meditation is the practice of focusing attention and awareness, and quieting your mind. Many people report that after meditating only fifteen minutes or so each day, they discover an inner clarity in which their deepest thoughts and feelings come to the surface, either during meditation itself or at other times of the day. Most yoga centers offer classes in meditation, and many spas do as well, as do schools and workplaces! Many find their home or car a perfect place to meditate. I recommend Sharon Salzberg's book *Lovingkindness,* which focuses on the practice of **metta meditation.**

- **Mind-body integration.** Forms of exercise that integrate mind and body—yoga, tai chi, and many forms of martial arts—are often a kind of moving meditation. These disciplines will make your body more flexible while helping to open your mind, heart, and spirit. They are an excellent way to recover your unique vision and reconnect to your deepest, truest perceptions.

- **Mindfulness practices.** Repeat a mantra or a phrase—a set of calming, inspirational words—while you are breathing. **I like Thich Nhat Hanh's "in out, deep slow, calm ease, smile release."** Focusing awareness on the present and being *still* on the inside brings more clarity of mind.

- **Treasure your time alone and protect it.** Our lives are so busy and scheduled that we often don't have time to connect with ourselves. The psychologist Thomas Moore compares the soul to a shy creature of the wild, suggesting that we must wait patiently by the side of the forest for it to emerge and share its wisdom. If you're feeling disconnected or confused, maybe all you need is some time to reconnect.

- **Spend time with trusted friends or family.** Sometimes, even in Stage 1 gaslighting, we find ourselves becoming increasingly isolated from everyone but our gaslighter. Even when we're not with them, we allow ourselves to become preoccupied with what they might say, think, wish, and demand. Hanging out with a person who sees you as you see yourself can be an excellent way to regain your own perspective.

Nothing can be accomplished without solitude. I have made a kind of solitude for myself which nobody is aware of.

—Pablo Picasso

Avoiding Stage 1 of the Gaslight Tango

Recognizing and avoiding the Gaslight Tango in Stage 1 gaslighting is an important step. *It's the only one of the three stages when you have the opportunity to not only stop the Gaslight Tango but avoid it altogether.*

How can you avoid the Gaslight Tango? Here are some suggestions.

With Your Date

- **Pay attention.** Be on the lookout for gaps between what you think is important and what they think is important.
- **Clarify your own thoughts and judgments.** If they seem to accuse you of something, ask yourself whether you agree with that assessment of your behavior.
- **Keep your sense of humor.** If they seem to be taking something far more seriously than you, hang on to your own sense of what's trivial, perhaps even absurdly so.
- **Do your best to stand up for yourself without engaging in an argument.** Often, when someone accuses you of something you find ridiculous, not saying anything is the best response. Trying to prove who's right and who's wrong is almost guaranteed to get the tango going.
- **Check in with your own feelings.** As the date proceeds, do you find yourself feeling annoyed? Anxious? Swept off your feet with delight? It may be too soon to tell what any of these feelings mean, but at least you can take notice of them.
- **Maintain a sense of perspective.** At the end of the date, check in with yourself to get your overall sense of how things went. If the good outweighs the

bad, you may want to see the person again, but allow yourself to remember anything that troubled or puzzled you.

With Your Boss

- **Identify the pattern.** Although your boss has gaslighted you, suggesting that you're emotionally unstable and unable to handle pressure, you don't yet know whether they engage in this type of gaslighting all the time or only in response to certain situations, such as when you make a mistake, do exceptionally well, or seem to be having difficulties. Knowing your boss's gaslight pattern can help you figure out what you can and cannot tolerate. It can also help you identify when the best time to interact with the person is.

- **Find out what your boss is willing to do.** Does the gaslighting inevitably result in punishment—altered work assignments, docked pay, dismissal—or is it only a psychological game? Again, when you see the situation clearly, you can decide on your own limits and have a conversation with your boss about what is and what isn't possible. It may be that they have no flexibility and continue to gaslight. In that case, leaving or setting limits will be your choice.

- **Figure out how much contact you need to have.** Some bosses are central parts of our working lives; others function more as offstage figures. No one likes to be gaslighted by a boss, but the behavior may be easier to endure if they play a relatively minor role in your day-to-day life at work.

With Your Family

- **Refuse to engage.** This is one of those "easy to say, hard to do" pieces of advice that you've probably heard many times before. Nevertheless, it's still the best way to keep from doing the Gaslight Tango with your mom, dad, brother, sister, or crabby aunt or cousin. With family, especially, the patterns are so established that they're very difficult to break. Refusing to engage in a gaslighting conversation is often the most powerful response of all.

- **Do your best to give up your investment in being seen as right.** If you need to be right, you're open to being gaslighted. I'm not saying you have to give up your deep, inner certainty that you are right. But as soon as you honestly don't care what your relatives think about your rightness, you'll be well on your way to freeing yourself from family gaslighting.

- **Let go of your commitment to being understood.** "I understand their point of view—why can't they understand mine?" It's hard to feel misunderstood, and even harder when it's your own family members who misunderstand you. But again, wanting to be understood leaves you wide open for gaslighting.

Stopping the Dance Once It Has Begun

How do you stop it? Here are some suggestions that are useful at any stage of gaslighting but are especially effective during **Stage 1.**

Don't Ask Yourself "Who's Right?" Ask Yourself "Do I Like Being Treated This Way?"

- As we've seen, one of the biggest hooks that keep us in gaslighting relationships is our need to be right. Worrying that we're not being fair, that we're too sensitive, or that we're making too big a deal of something can be a powerful silencer, leaving us vulnerable to another person's manipulations. But if we focus on how we are being treated, we cut through a lot of the confusion.

Don't Worry About Being "Good"—Just About Being "Good Enough"

- We desperately want to be seen as nice, kind, generous, nurturing, understanding, or responsive to a partner's need. Instead of thinking about how our partner is treating us, we put all our attention on how we behave. But it can also be a way to avoid seeing that our partner is treating us badly.

Don't Debate What You Know to Be True

- You want your partner to get the message that you're not open to argument about these topics. You know what's true, and you are not going to engage in ongoing discussions about it. Some things are not open for debate.

Always Tell Yourself the Truth about Yourself

- Your job is to resist criticism used as a weapon and maintain a true, balanced, and compassionate view of yourself. This is no easy task when you are faced with gaslighting, but it's essential to preserving your sense of self.

Reflection: Listen for Your Self-Talk—If your gaslighter says something like, "You're so forgetful," try to stop the dance before it begins. Ideally, your inner dialogue might follow one of these three patterns: *(Do any of these responses feel familiar?)*

☐ "Is he right? Am I really so forgetful? When was the last time I forgot something? You know, I can't think of a time. I think he's really over the top on this one!"

☐ "Is he right? Am I really so forgetful? When was the last time I forgot something? Well, I did forget to buy milk last week; maybe he's thinking of that. And I forgot to pick up the dry cleaning the week before. You know, two minor incidents don't add up to 'forgetful,' so I'm not going to worry about this."

☐ "Is he right? Well, of course he's right! I've been a forgetful person since I was five years old. I'm the original 'absentminded professor.' But so what? It's not okay for him to use my faults against me, and it's not okay for him to try to make me feel bad. I'm not going to focus on this one fault, and I don't want him to focus on it either. It's just not that big a deal, since I'm really good in so many other ways."

If you selected any of these options, well done—you have avoided stepping into the Gaslight Tango! The important thing is not who can win the argument, but how you want to be treated. Avoid the right–wrong debate.

Courage is the price that life exacts for granting peace.

—Amelia Earhart

Practice Opting Out of Arguments with Your Gaslighter

Things You Can Say to Avoid the Right–Wrong Debate

"You're right, but I don't want to keep arguing about this."

"You're right, but I don't want to be talked to that way."

"I'm happy to continue this conversation without name-calling."

"I'm not comfortable with where this conversation is going. Let's revisit it later."

"I think this conversation has gone as far as it can go."

"I don't think I can be constructive right now. Let's talk about this at another time."

"I think we have to agree to disagree."

"I don't want to continue this argument."

"I don't want to continue this conversation right now."

"I hear you, and I'm going to think about that. But I don't want to keep talking about it right now."

"I'd really like to continue this conversation, but I'm not willing to do so unless we can do it in a more pleasant tone."

"I don't like the way I'm feeling right now, and I'm not willing to continue this conversation."

"You may not be aware of it, but you're telling me that I don't know what reality is. And respectfully, I don't agree. I love you, but I won't talk to you about this."

> "I love having intimate conversations with you, but not when you're putting me down."
>
> "It may not be your intention to put me down, but I feel put down and I'm not going to continue the conversation."
>
> "This is not a good time for me to talk about this. Let's agree on another time that works for both of us."

Allow yourself permission to feel all your feelings, *but don't get drawn into an argument about your feelings or your right to be heard.*

Things You Can Say to Stop the Tango while Avoiding an Argument

"Please stop talking to me in that tone; I don't like it."

"I can't hear what you're really saying as long as you're yelling."

"I can't hear what you're really saying as long you're speaking to me with contempt."

"I don't want to talk while you're yelling at me."

"I don't want to talk while you're speaking to me with contempt."

"I am not going to continue this back-and-forth."

"From my point of view, you're distorting reality, and I really don't like it. I'll talk to you later when I'm feeling calmer."

"Perhaps you didn't intend to hurt my feelings, but I'm too upset to talk right now. We can talk about it later."

Choose one sentence that sums up what you want to say and then simply keep repeating that sentence. Choose the style that works best for you and your situation. Experiment until you find the right choice.

Making It Personal—In Your Own Words ...

What wording feels most like you? Write it down. Tweak it if necessary.

_____

_____

_____

_____

Now repeat it to yourself until you feel comfortable saying it, until it feels like you.

It can be very challenging to stop the Gaslight Tango. But most change happens in fits and starts. As long as you stick with it, you'll make progress. And if you're not making the kind of progress you'd like, consider finding a therapist, a support group, or some other type of help to give your efforts a boost.

Reflection: Choosing a Relationship—Now that we've explored **Stage 1 gaslighting,** let's reflect on our own relationships. Please choose a relationship you would like to focus on and answer the following questions as honestly as you can.

Take a few moments to describe the relationship you have chosen to focus on.

What does the Gaslight Tango look like in your relationship?

_____

_____

_____

_____

_____

Choose a specific gaslighting moment. What was your gaslighter's behavior?

_____

_____

_____

_____

What was your behavior?

_____

_____

_____

_____

Equipped with new knowledge and reflecting on your gaslighting dynamic, if the moment were to reoccur now, how could you gather your courage and opt out?

_____

_____

_____

_____

If you can stop the dance in **Stage 1**, while you're still relatively comfortable with your own view of things, you're way ahead of the game because you've avoided entering **Stage 2** or even **Stage 3**. As we'll see in the next chapter, stepping out of the tango becomes far more challenging once you're more deeply entrenched in trying to win your gaslighter's approval. The earlier you can opt out of this pattern, the better. The good news is that you have new knowledge, deeper insight, and new language to support you moving forward.

4

Stage 2:
"Maybe You Have a Point."

In this chapter, we will focus on the specific dynamics of **Stage 2** gaslighting and explore whether you are in any relationships with emerging **Stage 2** telltale signs. You might be wondering, "What's the difference? Don't all relationships contain a mix?"

You're absolutely right. Since relationships can contain a mixture of gaslighting dynamics, to various degrees, our objective is to focus on how **Stage 1, Stage 2,** and **Stage 3** dynamics differ—and how they evolve in our relationships.

Stage 1 Is Characterized by Disbelief

- You can't believe your partner is saying such silly things, making crazy accusations, or trying to tell you there's something wrong with you. Eventually, over time and with repetition, as your partner continues to insist on their reality and undermine yours, you begin to wonder and question if they can possibly be right. But at this stage you are still grounded in your own perspective.

Stage 2 Is Marked by the Need to Defend

- You are far more invested in defending yourself and winning your gaslighter's approval for being a good, capable, and lovable person—and they are even more invested in proving they're right. You are constantly defending yourself, ruminating over and over about what your partner said and what you said, and about who is right or wrong.

If you don't agree with your gaslighter, they might step up their version of the Emotional Apocalypse: yelling more loudly, finding more-pointed insults, giving you bigger doses of the silent treatment. When your gaslighter overreacts, you no longer wonder, "What's wrong with him?" Instead, you jump to placate him or to defend yourself.

Unexpected "Wow" Moments

A place to keep your spontaneous insights ... _____

_____

_____

_____

Have You Entered Stage 2? Are You ...

(Check the signs that feel familiar.)

- ☐ Not feeling quite as strong as you usually do?
- ☐ Seeing less of friends and loved ones?
- ☐ Agreeing less with people whose opinions you used to trust?
- ☐ Defending your gaslighter more and more often?
- ☐ Leaving out a lot of the way they talk to you and the way you feel with them when you describe the relationship?
- ☐ Making excuses for them to yourself and others?
- ☐ Ruminating about them constantly?
- ☐ Having more trouble thinking through past interactions in which the two of you disagreed?
- ☐ Obsessing, to yourself or others, about how you might have contributed to their anger, insecurity, withdrawal, or other unpleasant behavior?
- ☐ Frequently wondering whether you should have done something differently?
- ☐ Crying more?

☐ Plagued more often and/or more intensely by the vague feeling that something is wrong?

Telltale Sign—In Your Own Words . . .

As you review the items you checked, are you surprised by any of them?

_____

_____

Do you feel more concerned about certain items on the checklist in particular, or try to avoid thinking about them or their impact on your life? Spend a few minutes freewriting and unpacking the impact of these behaviors on your emotional life.

_____

_____

Which ones would you most like to change? How can you take a first step? What barriers might get in your way, and how can you best address them?

_____

_____

Your Relationship's River Story
Visualization

Now let's look at the relationship you are focusing on from a different perspective. I invite you to go through the River Story again, but this time it will be a River Story about your relationship. Look for touchstones and defining moments that might reflect whether and when you have entered a **Stage 2** gaslighting dynamic.

Allow yourself to reflect on your relationship from the first day you met to the present.

Your Journey

- Write the date when your relationship began in the bottom-left corner of a blank page and today's date in the upper-right corner.
- Next, draw the "river of your relationship" between the date you met and today's date. It can be a straight line, have many twists and turns, tributaries, or no tributaries—it's your decision.
- Now, close your eyes (if comfortable) or simply look down and imagine that you are on the bank of the river and getting into a hovercraft that will float two feet above the water. You will travel in this hovercraft following the river of your relationship from the beginning to the present date.
- As you float along, notice the touchstones beneath the water and allow them to represent those moments when your perception or feelings were either encouraged or crushed. Note those defining moments emblazoned in your memory.
- Write or draw those defining moments in your river and take a few minutes to notice those defining moments. What do you feel? What comes to your mind?

Defining Moments, Key Touchstones, and Feelings

Write or draw these defining moments and feelings that are emblazoned in your memory.

Now, take a step back and look at your relationship's River Story. Holding your key takeaways as we continue to explore Stage 2 gaslighting, please be open and gentle with yourself as your relationship continues to come into focus.

Self-discovery like climbing a mountain on a winding path. You keep coming across a view of the landscape before you, but each time you see it from a different perspective.

From Stage 1 to Stage 2

In Stage 1

- You'd like to win your gaslighter's approval and have them affirm what a good, capable, and lovable person you are, but you can live with the idea of not being able to do this. You begin with your own point of view, and when they say something that seems incorrect, you might argue.

Today's Date:

Beginning of your RELATIONSHIP:

- When they behave in a hurtful or bewildering manner, you wonder, "What's wrong with them?"
- You consider your own point of view to be normal and theirs (when they are gaslighting you) to be mistaken, distorted, or outrageous.
- You make judgments about what's going on and you're not sure you like someone who gets so upset about little things.

In Stage 2

- Winning your gaslighter's approval has become the only way you can feel confident that you're a good, capable, and lovable person.
- When they behave in a hurtful or bewildering manner, you wonder, "What's wrong with me?"
- You consider their point of view to be normal and fight desperately to get a hearing for your own perspective because you can't bear the idea that their

criticism of you may be true. You need to prove to this person that you are a good, capable, and lovable person by getting them to agree with you.

- You lose your ability to make judgments or to see the big picture, focusing instead on the details of their accusations and whether or not they are right.

UNDERSTANDING THE BEHAVIOR

From Stage 1 to Stage 2: Introduction to Attachment Theory (Anxious versus Secure)

As a child, your relational development started at birth. As a hardwired social-relational being, you immediately began to learn how relationships work and how to be in one.

How these early experiences unfold is crucial, because this developmental experience forms the foundation of your implicit understanding of how to be in a relationship and informs all of your future relationships.

For example, if you didn't feel loved, valued, or respected by your primary caregivers, this can create anxiety surrounding your ability to attach and connect to others.

If relational insecurity is learned in childhood, it can make you more susceptible to gaslighting as an adult. You have learned that anxiety and some manner of abuse are normal and acceptable. Behaviors, like seeking the other's approval and forfeiting your needs, are often learned to be the only way to stay emotionally safe and connected.

Taking It Deeper—The "Why"

From **Attachment Theory** we learn that early attachment experience will unfold with primary caregivers as either **secure** or **anxious**. This will depend on the degree to which the infant or child feels emotionally connected and safe with the primary caregivers.

These early relational experiences form what is known as your attachment style. Research indicates that we carry our attachment style into adult life, which unconsciously informs our adult relationships.

Before you had words, you lived in a relational world with your caregivers. This relational experience was both positive and negative for each of you. The repetitive nature *of this intersubjective dynamic* is encoded in your developing procedural/implicit memory. That is, it became your unconscious understanding of how relationships work, which psychologists refer to as **implicit relational knowing.**

Think of it as the procedural rule book (unconscious schema) we learn as children about how to be in a relationship. From the perspective of Attachment Theory, this phenomenon is referred to as the child's developing "internal working model" of relationships.

Finding Yourself—Take a Deeper Dive...
What Do You Believe About Relationships?

Who did you feel the safest with as a child? Why?

_____

_____

_____

Who did you feel the least safe with as a child? Why?

_____

_____

_____

How would you describe your relational attachment style with each of these people? (Is it Open/Trusting or Closed/Untrusting?)

_____

_____

Can you describe a relationship that you aspire to?

_____

_____

What is the most important quality for you in a love relationship?

_____

_____

What is the most important quality for you in a friendship or collegial relationship?

_____

_____

Are You Stuck in Stage 2?

"I'm Always on the Defensive"

Take the following quiz for more perspective.

Scenario 1—Your boyfriend takes you out to an elegant meal to celebrate your promotion, and you're thrilled. Then he says, "It's good to see you so relaxed and happy. For the past several weeks, you've just been snapping at me." Wondering what he is referring to and trying to stay calm, you ask him what he means. "You know," he says, "the other night when we went out, you asked me how you look and I was totally honest and told you that dress made you look a little fat. Even though I was telling the truth, you got so angry you wouldn't speak to me for most of dinner. You're just way, way too sensitive, aren't you?"

You respond:

a. ____ "Are you insane? Hasn't anyone ever told you how to talk to a woman?"

b. ____ "It's so hard to hear this. I just wanted to have a good time tonight. I'm willing to work on this issue, but can't I have one night off from the things I am working on?"

c. ____ "I'm sorry. I guess I should be more self-confident."

d. ____ "Whether you're right or not, I don't want to be criticized right now."

Scenario 2—You're on your way home, and you know your partner is waiting for you there.

You feel:

a. ___ Pleased to see them, though part of you wishes you could have dinner with friends.

b. ___ Pleased to see them but a bit nervous. They've been so touchy lately!

c. ___ Overcome with dread.

d. ___ Excited about seeing them, with no reservations.

Scenario 3—You're about to hand in an assignment late, and you know your boss will be angry. You had an excellent work record before they took over the department, but it's true: your work has been slipping ever since they came on board. Lately, they've been accusing you of trying to sabotage their leadership, and you're pretty sure they'll bring that up again. You begin to feel confused about how to respond.

You think:

a. ___ "I wonder if they're right. Maybe I am trying to sabotage them."

b. ___ "I don't think I'm trying to sabotage them—I've never done that to anyone before—but I have to admit, it does look pretty strange. I really don't think I have any hidden motive, but maybe there's something I'm not seeing."

c. ___ "I can't face them again without a Xanax."

d. ___ "My work is definitely not what it used to be. I just don't do well with this person's management style."

Scenario 4—You've been trying to diet, and everyone in the office knows it. Your colleague stops by your desk with some of her famous homemade muffins. You say politely, "Please, Anne. You know I'm dieting." Anne replies sweetly, "These are low-fat. And besides, a pretty woman like you doesn't need to diet." You insist: "Anne, I'm serious. If I start eating muffins, my whole eating plan will be thrown off." But she continues, "I've never seen anyone who had such a hard time accepting a little kindness! Maybe if you fed your emotions more, you'd have an easier time staying on your diet." Then she puts a muffin on your desk and walks away.

You think:

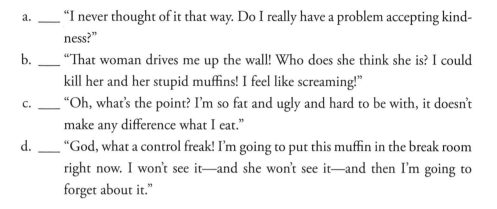

a. ___ "I never thought of it that way. Do I really have a problem accepting kindness?"

b. ___ "That woman drives me up the wall! Who does she think she is? I could kill her and her stupid muffins! I feel like screaming!"

c. ___ "Oh, what's the point? I'm so fat and ugly and hard to be with, it doesn't make any difference what I eat."

d. ___ "God, what a control freak! I'm going to put this muffin in the break room right now. I won't see it—and she won't see it—and then I'm going to forget about it."

Scenario 5—Your sister calls with a last-minute request for you to babysit. With her unerring instincts, she's picked the one night you happen to be free—a night you've been longing to spend at home. Somehow, you let it slip that you theoretically could accommodate her. "The kids will be so disappointed not to see you," she says. "And you did say I could call any time. I guess you like the idea of being an aunt more than the actual responsibilities. I guess that's why you don't have any children of your own. Well, if that's how you feel, you made the right decision."

You respond:

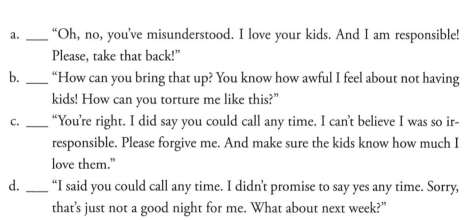

a. ___ "Oh, no, you've misunderstood. I love your kids. And I am responsible! Please, take that back!"

b. ___ "How can you bring that up? You know how awful I feel about not having kids! How can you torture me like this?"

c. ___ "You're right. I did say you could call any time. I can't believe I was so irresponsible. Please forgive me. And make sure the kids know how much I love them."

d. ___ "I said you could call any time. I didn't promise to say yes any time. Sorry, that's just not a good night for me. What about next week?"

Telltale Sign—Note which response you selected in each scenario. Did you pick one letter more than another?

Scenario 1:

Scenario 2:

Scenario 3:

Scenario 4:

Scenario 5:

Answer Key

If you answered "a" to most of these scenarios: You're responding at a Stage 1 level. You are seeking your gaslighter's approval but still maintaining your own perspective. Be careful, though. Stage 1 gaslighting often leads to Stage 2.

If you answered "b" to most of these scenarios: You seem to have entered Stage 2. You want so desperately to win your gaslighter's approval for being a good, capable, or lovable person that you have started to look at things from their perspective. You may be trying to defend yourself, but you invest a lot of energy into arguing with them, hoping to prove to yourself that their dire criticisms really aren't true. In a way, you've already let them win simply by letting them into your head.

If you answered "c" to most of these scenarios: It sounds like you're not even defending yourself anymore, just trying to endure defeat. Although you'd like to win your gaslighter's approval, you've almost given up hope that you ever will. If this is really how you feel, you've moved past Stage 2 and into Stage 3. You might want to skip ahead to the next chapter.

If you answered "d" to most of these scenarios: Congratulations! You're keeping a firm grip on reality, resisting the Urge to Merge, and opting out of arguments rather than trying to prove you're right. You may care about your gaslighter, but you can live without their approval because you know that you are a good, capable, and lovable person, no matter what they (or anyone else) think. Just being able to imagine this type of response is a big step forward.

The Three Types of Gaslighters in Stage 2

Each type of gaslighter tends to escalate their gaslighting in a different way and is likely to have their own version of **Stage 2** gaslighting.

Intimidator Gaslighters

Behavior Examples—In Stage 2, the Intimidator is likely to bring out the heavy artillery. They may employ one or more of the following tactics as their Emotional Apocalypse:

- Yelling
- Guilt-tripping
- Belittling
- Giving the silent treatment
- Threatening to leave
- Making dire predictions ("You're never going to pass the bar exam. You're just not smart enough; it's stupid to even try.")
- Playing on your worst fears ("You're just like your mother!")

Some save the worst treatment for group situations or are kind and attentive in public but bring out the insults in private. Or it could be a mix of both.

Telltale Sign—In Your Own Words . . .

Is there something you have experienced that is not on the list? Please reflect on your personal experiences, thoughts, and feelings. How would you describe them? Do a freewrite and go as deep and into as much detail as you want.

_____

_____

_____

_____

Intimidator Relational Dynamics

- The gaslighter urgently needs to be right, no matter the topic.
- Their Emotional Apocalypse is a terrifying combination of yelling, insults, and reckless behavior that leaves the gaslightee scared and confused.
- Urge to Merge—You are still hoping for a way to find complete agreement.
- Gaslight Tango—You are still trying to show your gaslighter that they've misunderstood you and should think about you differently.

You can fight back, but it doesn't stop the gaslighting. They're still invested in being right, and you're still invested in winning their approval. Arguments don't change that. And even if you win, you've still given them power over your self-image. So you continue to fight, needing them to affirm how good, capable, and lovable you are.

Resist the Urge to Merge and Opt Out of the Fight—Opting out of the fight doesn't necessarily get your gaslighter to behave any better. But at least you're holding on to your sense of self and integrity. You're focused on what you want. If you stay committed to opting out and stick to what you've said you want and will do, they may reconsider their behavior.

Reflection—Making It Personal

Have you had a similar experience? Can you remember how you felt during your exchange?

_____

_____

_____

Holding the memory of that feeling, what would you say to opt out and end the exchange in a clear and productive way?

_____

_____

_____

Glamour Gaslighters

Glamour Gaslighters may be harder to identify. In Stage 2, your Glamour Gaslighter may have you convinced that the problem isn't them; it's your inability to accept happiness, to be more flexible, or to tolerate ordinary imperfections. This type of gaslighter is not really responding to you and your concerns. They're just as concerned as the Intimidator with being right, but they put up a very attractive smokescreen.

Behavior Examples

- They sweep you off your feet with a dozen roses but often show up three hours late or refuse to be pinned down to any arrival time at all. When you complain, they accuse you of being controlling, paranoid, or unspontaneous.
- They're constantly surprising you with romantic gestures, though they often don't key into what you're actually feeling. But they seem so pleased with their efforts that you keep wondering what's wrong with you for not having a better time.
- They alternate between the most remarkable responsiveness (mental, emotional, sexual) and the most blatant insensitivity. When they're being responsive, you're ecstatic; when they're not, you blame yourself.
- They're generous and giving, but periodically they explode in a rage, withdraw into an icy silence, or collapse into a childish misery. Although they refuse to blame you directly, you're sure it's your fault, though you can never quite figure out what you did.
- When you're together, life is wonderful, but then there are those little details that don't quite add up. For some Glamour Gaslighters, the problem is money (e.g., your cash keeps going missing). For others, it could be a sexual issue (e.g., when they're distant and evasive, you're sure they're cheating on you). Then they sweep you back into a romantic embrace, and you wonder why you're being so paranoid.

You may be nodding in recognition, yet still feeling confused. Let me tell you why.

Glamour Gaslighting Relational Dynamics

- The gaslighter is completely involved in proving to themself what a romantic person they are.
- It looks like they're relating to you, but they're only involved with themself.
- Their actions may appear to be loving, attentive, and satisfying, but their lack of genuine connection leaves you feeling lonely.
- You blame yourself, not your partner, for the annoyance and confusion you feel.
- You're likely to adopt their perspective, not your own.
- You may even convince yourself that you are uptight, conventional, and demanding.

To opt out of this Glamour Gaslighting Tango, you'll have to be willing to give up some goodies. If you want the behavior to change, you have to have faith in yourself to stick with your own feelings.

Reflection—Making It Personal

Have you had a similar experience? Can you remember how you felt during your exchange?

_____

_____

_____

Holding the memory of that feeling, what could you say to opt out or end the exchange in a clear way?

_____

_____

_____

Good-Guy Gaslighters

In Stage 2, the Good-Guy Gaslighters present a confusing picture. It looks like they're being cooperative, pleasant, and helpful, but you still end up feeling confused and frustrated. See if any of these scenarios sound familiar.

Behavior Examples

- One minute, he's giving you the perfect advice about how to handle your mother; the next, he has a blank look on his face when you want to continue the conversation. When you ask what caused the freeze out, he either won't tell you or assures you there isn't a problem.
- You argue for hours over a specific concern, then suddenly he'll end the argument by giving in and doing exactly as you've asked. Perhaps he doesn't seem really satisfied, but you've gotten your way, so how can you complain? Despite this apparent generosity, you feel tricked. When he gives in, you feel that it's not so much because he cares about your feelings, but because he wants to prove what a good guy he is. You end up thinking you must be crazy, ungrateful, or incapable of being satisfied, because after all, he is such a great guy.
- He'll do his share and more of the household and relationship work. Yet you never quite feel as though he's fully participating. When you ask for emotional reassurance or try to connect with him more deeply, he'll look at you blankly. Why, you wonder, are you so selfish and demanding?

As you can see, the Good-Guy Gaslighter finds a way to make it look like he's doing everything you want—without ever really giving you what you want.

Good-Guy Gaslighting Relational Dynamics

- The gaslighter engages in "disrespectful compliance," going through the motions of agreeing while finding all sorts of little ways to show how unhappy and resentful they feel.
- The gaslighter's Emotional Apocalypse is pouting, withdrawing, or sulking.
- The gaslighter tries to make themself look like a good guy instead of being clear about what they want and need.

- You think everything is fine. Yet you often find yourself crying, lonely, stressed out, confused, or numb.
- You worry about their approval, idealize the gaslighter, and tend to take their perspective over your own sense of reality.

Reflection—Making It Personal

Have you had a similar experience with a Good-Guy Gaslighter? Do you remember how you felt?

_____

_____

_____

A Different Approach

Let's see what happens when you stop worrying about the Good-Guy's approval, refuse to idealize him, and hold on to your own reality, even in the face of his need to always be right. You don't object in words, but your actions speak for you.

Response Options

Instead of self-blaming, try to see the situation clearly. For example, saying, "I am so afraid it could be my fault" isn't helping you. Instead, try the clear-sighted approach: "My husband is being dishonest about his feelings and pouting (or having a tantrum or guilt-tripping me or insulting me) when he doesn't get his way, and I don't like that!"

- Now you're **opting out of the argument.** You're refusing to debate what you know to be true. You are relying on your own sense of truth, not on what he says is true.
- You're **refusing to fear** his Emotional Apocalypse and his veiled threat of withdrawing his love.
- **Resisting the Urge to Merge.** You're not trying to convince your husband to agree with you to win his approval.
- You're simply making your own decision and sticking with your own reality.

Stage 2: The Explanation Trap

As a reminder, the Explanation Trap is *any effort to explain away behavior that disturbs us,* or makes us uncomfortable, including gaslighting. In an effort to control the situation, we find seemingly rational explanations to prove to ourselves why these danger signals aren't really dangerous.

Example—Naomi responds intellectually in an effort to analyze "the problem of Douglas." Why is he behaving in such a difficult, demanding way? What is behind his need to insult her or stop speaking to her? He presents a fascinating character study, which results in her objectifying Douglas and distancing herself from a deeper, more intimate connection.

Naomi believes if she were to respond emotionally to her experience, she might get sucked into a quagmire, lose control, and quickly tire of being treated disrespectfully and with such little regard.

But she has kept herself interested in the relationship by thinking about it, because his abusive aspects offered so many opportunities to come up with explanations for Douglas as well as herself.

With a nicer, more reliable person, the relationship doesn't offer as much food for thought. *So, like many women involved in Stage 2 gaslighting, Naomi seemed to be more interested in the drama and analysis involved in a bad relationship than in the relatively mundane experience of a good one, where she might get too comfortable and bored.*

Check In with Your Reality—Why do some people become so excited about analyzing their gaslighters? I've come to believe there are two reasons.

1. Dealing with an unpredictable person can make us feel more alive and connected.
2. Trying to understand a gaslighter can make us feel more in control.

We believe that the more we can control, the more we can be sure of, and the less we can be hurt by an unreliable parent, friend, or lover who fails or disappoints us.

In Your Own Words…

Does trying to analyze your gaslighter leave you feeling more in control or more caught up in drama? Do you find it compelling?

_____

_____

_____

_____

What else could be your reason?

_____

_____

_____

_____

UNDERSTANDING THE BEHAVIOR

Are You Stuck in the Explanation Trap? The Need to Explain Away Bad Behavior

For many adults with an insecure attachment style and sense of self, the nature of loving or needing another can be synonymous with a fear of dependency, disappointment, and **giving up control**. This represents a terrifying proposition, especially if it means exposing your vulnerable feeling self to rejection and manipulation.

An **insecure attachment style** can manifest in adults as a strategy to create emotional distance from their partner. This "safety in distance" can unconsciously feel like a protective shield around you and your feelings of vulnerability.

Unfortunately, the very nature of relationships involves some loss of control. However, focusing on the Explanation Trap (rather than your true feelings) can create a false sense of safety and give us the illusion of having more control than we do.

You may need to accept that your partner's behavior is completely beyond your control. All you can do is pause and decide on your own response to whatever the other chooses to give you.

How do you free yourself from the **Explanation Trap**? First, focus on your emotional responses and allow yourself to feel whatever you're feeling. Be on the lookout for your Flight Attendants (page 52). As we move forward, we will explore more options for what you can do.

Taking It Deeper—The "Why"

"Insecure Attachments into Adulthood" (Attachment Theory)

For a person with an insecure attachment style, maintaining distance from one's vulnerable feelings can create a false sense of emotional safety.

The unconscious inner dialogue may sound like this: *"Getting too close and needing too much is dangerous. I don't really need the other to survive."*

This may also create a false sense of control by unconsciously protecting your vulnerable feeling self from the feared re-creation of childhood trauma (e.g., rejection/negative mirroring/disappointment/ invasion of personal boundaries, etc.).

In effect, this emotional distance limits our ability to be more intuitive, empathic, and emotionally connected to the other.

Emotional distancing can become a habitual, unconscious strategy that requires a great deal of psychic energy to maintain control and protect yourself from "needing" the other.

Finding Yourself—Take a Deeper Dive...
What Is Your Explanation?

What is your gaslighter's behavior that you need to explain away?

_____

_____

_____

_____

_____

What is your explanation to yourself? What is your explanation to others?

_____

_____

_____

_____

Does your explanation help mitigate your negative feelings and fears?

_____

_____

_____

What is _your_ behavior that you need to explain away?

_____

_____

_____

What is your explanation to yourself? What is your explanation to others?

_____

_____

_____

Does your explanation help mitigate your unspoken or unresolved fears?

_____

_____

_____

Do you think you may have distanced yourself from yourself, the other, or both? How?

_____

_____

_____

If you have, how might you imagine reconnecting with your inner truth?

_____

_____

_____

Stage 2: The Negotiation Trap

The **Negotiation Trap** is another version of the **Explanation Trap.** It's especially common among those involved with Good-Guy Gaslighters.

Those of us caught in the **Negotiation Trap** tend to focus not on the overall satisfaction that a relationship brings us, but on our success or lack of success in negotiating with our partner. We actually find the power struggle exciting. But the very negotiations that once made you feel energized and strong now leave you feeling unhappy, weak, and exhausted.

It looks as though your partner is being cooperative and responsive, but in fact, their negotiations become a way of ignoring your concerns while trying to convince you that they are really paying attention. You may end up feeling that you have to keep the performance going, pretending to negotiate when what you really want is to weep in frustration.

Because of the Good Guy's willingness to negotiate, you may come to believe you have no grounds for complaint. But you feel lonely, bewildered, and numb.

The gaslightee had been involving herself in these negotiations to avoid her very real and very uncomfortable feelings about her gaslighter and their relationship. It was a way of not having to face how frustrated, lonely, and ignored she felt.

Check In with Your Reality—Negotiations can be enormously productive, but be careful not to let the negotiation process blind you to your own emotional reality. All that matters is your own deepest, most authentic sense of inner truth. Allow yourself to experience the totality of your relationship and then turn to the next exercise to figure out what you'd like to do next.

Finding Your Inner Truth
Clarifying Techniques for Stage 2 Gaslighting

1. **Write down a troubling or confusing dialogue** (as close to verbatim as you can) that you had with your gaslighter and take a few minutes to look at it.

Now that you're not actually engaged in the conversation with your gaslighter, how do they sound to you?

_____ Reasonable?

_____ Helpful?

_____ Unexpected or odd?

_____ Like an obstructionist?

_____ Something else?

Please take a minute to reflect on your thoughts and feelings about what you noticed.

2. **Talk to a trusted friend or mentor.** Share your gaslighter's criticisms and concerns with a friend. (Trust me, the people who know you best know all your faults!) They should be able to help you get some perspective.

Your gaslighter may be very skilled at turning a genuine issue into a completely distorted portrait. For example, you might indeed have a chronic (and annoying) problem with lateness. But that doesn't mean your difficulties with being on time are a deliberate attempt to humiliate your gaslighter. They may have the right to be annoyed with you. But that doesn't entitle them to make wild accusations, like the following statements:

- "You like being late—just to drive me crazy."
- "You deliberately keep me waiting to torture me!"

- "Believe me, all of our friends are talking about it; they can't believe how badly you treat me."
- "You have a serious problem with money. Don't you get it?"
- "You love to flaunt your close friendships in my face. Are you trying to make me jealous all the time?"

A friend or mentor can help you regain your sense of proportion (e.g., "Well, you are often late, and it is annoying. But I don't think you're doing it to get back at Joe; it's the way you are with everybody!").

List your gaslighter's criticisms and accusations. To prepare and clarify your thoughts, write them down here . . .

My Gaslighter's Accusations . . .

_____

_____

_____

_____

_____

_____

Step back and look at the list. Now, being your own best friend, check the ones that you admit have some grain of truth.

Reflecting on the ones you checked (and being as honest as you can), get in touch with your real thoughts, motivations, and needs surrounding your behavior. Can you separate your truth from the false accusation of your gaslighter? Now, write those realizations down.

The Distortion (Not True)

_____

_____

_____

_____

_____

_____

My Truth, My Real Motivations, and My Needs . . .

_____

_____

_____

_____

_____

_____

Example—Whenever my gaslighter was late for dinner and I complained or told him how I felt, he told me that I'm the one with big issues around being on time. **Truth**—He's right! Being on time is important to me. It is respectful and considerate and a way to let people know you value their time. **Distortion (not true)**—He says time is a ridiculous construct and the average person is way too uptight about it, and I have these issues because my parents were overly concerned about it.

3.   **Pay rigorous attention to your feelings.** Often when you're with a gaslighter, you can't cut through the fog of verbal and emotional abuse. You may not be able to think your way to clarity while you're talking. But you can always say, "I don't like the way I feel. Let's continue at another time" and cut the interaction short.

Talk to your gaslighter on your own terms and on an agreed-upon timetable, not just on their timetable, and let your feelings tell you when you've had enough.

When you've lost touch with your feelings and feel destabilized in the interaction, what could you say to your gaslighter to end the conversation? Write it down and then say it out loud to practice what it feels like to stand your ground in the face of adversity.

_____

_____

_____

_____

4.   **Reflect on your feelings first.** Now, reflecting back on the exchange with your gaslighter, can you get in touch with what you were really feeling? What might have gotten in the way of your ability to express yourself clearly in the moment?

I was feeling . . .

_____

_____

_____

_____

5.   **Go away for a weekend—or just out for a cup of coffee.** Sometimes, you just need some time—or space—away from your gaslighter to realize how crazy and intolerable the situation has become. If you can spend some time with a friend or someone with whom you feel emotionally safe—someone you trust who makes you feel good about yourself—so much the better. Experiencing the contrast between how well things work in a safe, comfortable relationship and how confused, hurt, and frustrated you feel with your gaslighter should help you see your gaslighting relationship more clearly.

List places you want to go and people you want to see. Plan your time away now, so you don't feel helpless or confused in the moment.

_____

_____

_____

_____

_____

_____

6.   **Insist on your own perceptions.** I recommend having a sentence that says—to both you and your gaslighter—that you own your own perceptions and express them with authority.

Here are a few suggestions.

- "I know you feel that way, but I don't agree with you."
- "I see things differently."
- "That is your perception, but mine is different."

Freeing Yourself from Stage 2

As we've seen, the difference between Stage 1 and Stage 2 is the difference between *isolated incidents* and *consistent behavior.*

- **In Stage 1,** occasional gaslighting moments occur; these are moments that you can often identify and remember.
- **In Stage 2,** gaslighting has become your reality, the defining character of your relationship. Just as a fish doesn't know it's in water, you no longer see yourself in an unusual situation.

Now, you've begun to regain your awareness. Whether you're dealing with a partner, relative, friend, colleague, or boss, you're ready to take some action and make changes.

How Do You Begin?

Here are some suggestions for breaking free from Stage 2 gaslighting.

1.   **Take It Slow**—Find one small, specific step to begin with, like "opting out" of arguments, using short, simple statements that don't invite response.

What Are Your Barriers?

What is your initial reaction when I talk about taking it slow but "taking action"?

_____

_____

_____

_____

What are the barriers inside of you? *For example: "I don't feel comfortable not saying anything."*

_____

_____

_____

_____

What are the barriers outside of you? *For example: "I'm afraid of my partner's anger if I don't respond."*

_____

_____

_____

_____

Opting-Out Statements
- Take a deep breath and say nothing.
- "We're going to have to agree to disagree."
- "We're going to have to agree to disagree. I really don't want to continue this conversation."

- Refuse to answer rather than give in to your desire to reassure your partner.
- "Let's talk about this when it's not so heated between us, I just can't do it now."

You have to learn to go against your habitual impulses and train your behavior in another direction. Instead of begging for your gaslighter's approval—which may make them even more anxious or angry—you have to find ways of opting out of the argument.

In Your Own Words . . .

Can you think of some opt-out statements that feel more personal to your relationship?

Please write them down.

_____

_____

_____

_____

_____

_____

Now **repeat** the words out loud until you feel comfortable saying them. You can continue to tweak them to feel more comfortable. You may want to change a few words after you've started practicing opting out.

2.   **Find the Right Time**—Try to find a good time to talk with your gaslighter, free from situations or people that might trigger high anxiety. If you can, plan on when and how to raise your concerns rather than simply blurting them out. You may be surprised at how much better the conversation goes.

• **Old You**—In your own words, what would you have said? _____

_____

_____

_____

_____

_____

_____

_____

The following are some example sentences you could use once you are more comfortable opting out.

✔ Take a deep breath and say, "I'd like to talk to you about something. Is now a good time?"

✔ "When would be a good time to talk? It's important to me."

✔ "Okay, I'm not going to talk about this right now. If you want to finish watching the game, you can." Then leave the room.

✔ "It seems like right now might not be the best time to talk about this—we're both distracted by our phones. Let's revisit the conversation at a more relaxed time for both of us." Both of you should suggest possible times.

• **New You**—In your own words, what could you say to opt out of an argument and talk later? _____

_____

_____

You may not trust yourself to not fall back into your old pattern: If you keep arguing, your gaslighter will simply wear you out with logic, put-downs, and dismissiveness. But it can be empowering to tell them straight out that their comments hurt your feelings, or to simply end the conversation because it's going nowhere or hurting you.

3.   **Raise the Issue You Want to Discuss in a Blame-Free Way**—Nothing is guaranteed to provoke a fight faster than telling someone, "You always do such-and-such" or "You're attacking me" or "You're behaving badly." Instead, tell your gaslighter that you're not comfortable with what's going on between the two of you right now.

- **Old You**—In your own words, what would you have said in a blaming way?

  _____

  _____

  _____

  _____

- **New You**—In your own words, what would you say in a blame-free way?

  _____

  _____

  _____

  _____

4.   **Say What You Will and Won't Do**—If you say you are going to behave in a certain way, it's important that you be committed and consistent. Don't make empty threats or back down when your gaslighter steps up the intimidation, manipulation, or romantic gestures. Opting out of the argument is the only way. Engaging in the fight will only prolong the gaslighting.

- **Old You**—In your own words, what would you have said to gain your gaslighter's approval? _____

  _____

  _____

  _____

  _____

- **New You**—In your own words, what would you say to give you both time to process and act differently? _____

  _____

  _____

  _____

  _____

5. **Stand Your Ground**—If your gaslighter responds to your concerns with an attack, simply repeat your intention: "I don't want to be talked to that way anymore, and I won't stay in the room if it happens." If necessary, end the conversation yourself: "I've said what I have to say, and I don't want to argue about it. I know you've heard me, and now I'm going into another room. I don't want to continue talking now."

- **Old You**—In your own words, what would you have said to give into your gaslighter's attacks? _____

    _____

    _____

    _____

- **New You**—In your own words, what would you say to stand your ground in a more assertive manner? _____

    _____

    _____

    _____

Breaking free from **Stage 2** is a real challenge, because:

1. The relationship has now become defined according to its gaslighting dynamic.
2. Efforts to opt out of Stage 2 can result in a genuinely healthy relationship. However, it can also bring about a new version of Stage 1 in which your partner periodically tries to gaslight you and you occasionally go along with it.

But the effort is worth it. As painful as it can be, it's much easier to deal with than the total, overwhelming dynamic of Stage 3 gaslighting. You might be wondering, "How will I know when the relationship isn't salvageable anymore and it's time to get out?" We will discuss this and what you can do in detail in chapter 7, "Should I Stay or Should I Go?"

5

Stage 3: "It's All My Fault!"

Depression

In this chapter, we will focus on the specific dynamics of **Stage 3** gaslighting. This is the phase in which you have assimilated your gaslighter's perspective and taken it on as your own.

It's critically important to recognize when Stage 2 begins to blend into Stage 3, because this is a phase in which gaslighting victims are often more isolated and experiencing abuse, like being yelled at, taken advantage of, and otherwise exploited.

Unexpected "Wow" Moments

A place to keep your spontaneous insights . . .

_____

_____

_____

_____

_____

Stage 1—You marshal evidence against your gaslighter, trying to show them that they're wrong. You may or may not fear their Emotional Apocalypse, but you definitely feel the Urge to Merge.

Stage 2—You argue with them and with yourself more desperately. You're more afraid of their Emotional Apocalypse and feel a more urgent sense of the Urge to Merge. You try harder to make your points align.

Stage 3—You've adopted your gaslighter's point of view and are marshaling evidence on their behalf.

Have You Entered Stage 3? Do You . . .

(Check the signs that feel all too familiar.)

- ☐ Frequently feel listless, apathetic, or lackluster?
- ☐ Find it virtually impossible to spend time relaxing with friends and loved ones?
- ☐ Find it virtually impossible to make decisions on your own?
- ☐ Avoid meaningful conversations with people whose opinions you trust?
- ☐ Continually defend your gaslighter to others and yourself?
- ☐ Avoid all mention of the relationship so you don't have to make others understand?
- ☐ Often find yourself crying for seemingly no reason?
- ☐ Experience stress-related symptoms, such as migraines, upset stomach, constipation or diarrhea, hemorrhoids, hives, acne or rashes, backaches, or other disorders?
- ☐ Frequently suffer from minor or major illnesses, such as colds, flu, colitis, digestive problems, heart palpitations, shortness of breath, asthma attacks, or other disorders?
- ☐ Find yourself unable to clearly remember an interaction in which you and your gaslighter disagreed?
- ☐ Obsess—to yourself or others—about how you might have contributed to your gaslighter's anger, insecurity, withdrawal, or other unpleasant behavior?
- ☐ Feel increasingly plagued by the vague sense that something is wrong?

Reflection

Now that we have begun to explore **Stage 3 gaslighting**, let's reflect on your own relationships. Is there one you would like to focus on to answer the following questions?

_____

_____

Do any of these signs feel familiar to you? Are you surprised?

_____

_____

How often do these types of feelings or behaviors happen and to what degree?

_____

_____

Can you remember when you didn't feel or behave this way?

_____

_____

Your Relationship's River Story: Stage 3

Visualization

Spend the next few minutes thinking about the relationship you are focusing on from a different perspective. I invite you to return to your relationship's River Story (see page 76) to look for touchstones and defining moments that might indicate whether it has entered a **Stage 3** gaslighting dynamic.

Allow yourself to reflect on your relationship from the first day you met to the present.

1. Write the date when your relationship began in the bottom-left corner of a blank page and today's date in the upper-right corner.

2. Next, draw the "river of your relationship" between the date you met and to-day's date. It can be a straight line, have many twists and turns, tributaries, or no tributaries—it's your decision.

3. Now, close your eyes (if comfortable), or simply look down, relax, and take a few long deep breaths to release your current self-state.

4. As you float along, two feet above your flowing river in your personal hover-craft, look into the water for touchstones, the defining moments that have shaped your relationship for better or worse. Moments when your reality-perception-feelings were **encouraged** by your partner (family member, friend, colleague) or when they were **squashed or dismissed**. Write down the **impact** those moments had on your **self-perception** and on your **behavior in the relationship and in general**.

5. At any time, you can add those moments (either through writing or drawing) to your river.

6. When your River Story feels complete, go back to the beginning and allow yourself to float way up into the sky in a hot-air balloon. Retracing your jour-ney from this higher perspective, see which **one or two defining moments** leap out. Focus on **the feelings that emerge** as you recall those moments and add those feelings to your river.

Defining Moments, Key Touchstones, and Feelings

Add the defining moments and feelings that are emblazoned in your memory, either through writing or drawing.

Now, take a step back and look at your relationship's River Story. Holding your key takeaways as we continue to explore Stage 3 gaslighting, please be open and gentle with yourself as your relationship comes into focus.

Notes: Write down the key moments you remember during your transition from Stage 2 to Stage 3, and what kind of impact those moments had on you.

- What do you feel as you look at this river of defining moments between you and your gaslighter that led to your being in Stage 3 now?

From the perspective of your hot-air balloon, reflect on what else was going on in your life during those key transitional moments. Consider . . .

Today's Date:

Beginning of your RELATIONSHIP:

- Did other events in your life have an impact on your transition from Stage 2 to Stage 3? If yes, what were those events?
- How did those events impact your relationship specifically?
- How do you think moving into Stage 3 might have impacted what else was happening in your life?

The Differences between Stage 2 and Stage 3

Stage 2

- You really want to win your gaslighter's approval, so you begin with their point of view.
- When they behave in a hurtful or bewildering manner, you wonder, "What's wrong with me?"
- You consider their point of view normal and fight desperately to get a hearing

for your own perspective. You want to prove the one thing that really matters to you: that you are a good, capable, loveable person. However, you can only prove this when this person agrees that you are.

- You lose your ability to make judgments, focusing instead on the details of their accusations.

Stage 3

- You want to win your gaslighter's approval but feel hopeless about being able to do so.
- You can't disengage because you feel depressed or apathetic, so it's a struggle to have a point of view at all. You no longer feel moved to defend yourself or to share your ideas.
- When your gaslighter behaves in a hurtful or bewildering manner, you are sure it must be your fault or if you believe it isn't your fault, you feel numb, disconnected, or hopeless.
- You consider your gaslighter's point of view normal. You may try to silence your perspective to align with theirs. You have many answers to your frequent question: "What's wrong with me?"
- You aren't challenging their perceptions in any way, whether it's the big picture or the details.

Stage 3: When Defeat Feels Normal

- Your transition to Stage 3 may pass imperceptibly. One of the greatest dangers of Stage 3 is your increased loss of perspective. Feeling defeated, hopeless, and joyless may come to feel normal.
- You may want to avoid the people and relationships that could "bring you back to life." Since staying in a gaslighting relationship demands that you remain shut down, interacting with your loved ones may feel too painful.
- Stage 3 gaslighting is truly soul-destroying. It is described as a listlessness that spreads through almost every area of one's life. To me, the worst aspect of Stage 3 is the hopelessness.
- You idealize your gaslighter and wish desperately for their approval. But you've given up on getting it and, as a result, you think the worst of yourself.

The Three Types of Gaslighters in Stage 3

Intimidator Gaslighters: Relationship Dynamics

The Intimidator Gaslighter rages, insults, and belittles.

- The Urge to Merge is apparent when you imagine the other to be in tune with your own values and judgments.
- Because you depend on the other for your sense of self, you are vulnerable to their opinions.
- You choose to blame yourself because you need your gaslighter's approval.
- If you could find a way to let your gaslighter's approval matter less—to judge yourself rather than let them judge you—you could free yourself from the gaslighting.

Glamour Gaslighters: Relationship Dynamics

The Glamour Gaslighter puts on a show for their own benefit while trying to convince you that it's all for your benefit. They enjoy it. You don't.

- While it looks like your gaslighter is being a great partner, they aren't really connecting with you or providing the intimacy and companionship you want.
- Your gaslighter puts on a big show, but their behavior leaves you feeling unsatisfied and unable to complain.
- Your gaslighter is insisting that you enjoy their show, but not checking to see if you really are. And the truth is, you aren't.
- You feel as though it is your fault and fear the Emotional Apocalypse and the resulting guilt.
- You feel nothing you can do will make a difference anymore and you can't imagine what will make you happy. You feel flat and numb.

Good-Guy Gaslighters: Relationship Dynamics

The Good-Guy Gaslighter knows how to get their own way while convincing you that you're getting your way.

- Your gaslighter is withholding a part of themselves while trying to convince you that they're giving their all.
- You feel lonely, confused, and frustrated, but can't say why.

- If you object, your gaslighter evokes the Emotional Apocalypse: They might yell, threaten to leave you, or barrage you with criticism.
- At no point have your feelings really been considered, but at every point you've been asked to believe that they have.

In **Stage 3** you may not even be aware of how essential it is to stop and look—not only at where you are now, but at where you were when you first met this person. Sometimes all you can do is breathe and remember who you were before you gave up pieces of yourself to gain your gaslighter's approval. Sometimes it is too painful to think of a way to restore yourself—you simply don't have the strength you used to have.

If this resonates with you, know that there is hope. And more than that, there is a pathway. The first step is to connect more deeply with yourself. There are a few meditation techniques you can try, like the one described here. This is the first step.

Metta Meditation: Sending Lovingkindness to Yourself and Others

May I be happy of mind.
May I be healthy of body.
May I be free of suffering.
May I have ease of well-being.
—Sharon Salzberg, from her book *Lovingkindness*

Meditation Can Help

- Find a quiet place where you won't be distracted or interrupted. It's a good idea to create this kind of space in your home so that you always have a place to retreat to. It can be a part of a room or simply a quiet corner.
- When you are ready, get comfortable in your seat—use a cushion, pillow, chair, or a mat on the floor. Begin breathing in and out. Slow deep belly breaths work well for meditation. As you breathe in, hold the thought, the first phrase of the meditation, **"May I be happy of mind."** Breathe out.

- Breathe in. **"May I be healthy of body."** Breathe out. Continue the breathing cycle with **"May I be free of suffering"** and **"May I have ease of well-being."**
- This meditation consists of five parts. First, send compassion to yourself. Then, send the same wishes to someone you love, to someone neutral in your life, to someone you are struggling with, and then back to yourself. I recommend repeating this meditation three times.

Bring your full open presence to the meditation and you will feel the warmth of compassion and lovingkindness.

Access Your "Deepest Self": Mind-Body Work

- Reconnect to yourself through mind-body activity: yoga, tai chi, martial arts, or other forms of moving meditation. Quiet your mind and open to your deepest self through movement that integrates body, mind, and spirit.

- You may prefer to meditate. In meditation, you can sit for five, ten, or fifteen minutes—or longer if you want—focusing on your breathing or a phrase or mantra instead of your thoughts. Give your deepest self the time and space to make itself heard. Meditation can help you feel calmer, more connected, and more able to handle stress.

One of the hardest aspects of Stage 3 gaslighting is the way it makes you feel disconnected from your emotions and the stronger self you used to be.

Check out appendix D for more self-care suggestions (page 263).

You'll never find a rainbow if you're looking down.

—Charlie Chaplin

WHY DO WE STAY?

Six Major Reasons

The Threat of Violence

Warning

People who reach Stage 3 sometimes fear—or may have even experienced—physical violence or the threat of physical violence from their gaslighter.

If you or your children have been physically assaulted, or if you believe you might be, *leave your home and go somewhere safe—the home of a loved one, a shelter, or even a restaurant*—where you can make phone calls and decide on your next step. *Your first concern needs to be protecting your physical safety and your children's.* The emotional dynamics can be worked out only when you know you and your children are safe and will remain so.

1. **Material Concerns**—Many women don't want to give up the economic security or standard of living that their gaslighting partner or boss can provide. Many women also feel that if there are children involved, they would suffer in the event of a divorce. Sometimes we perceive these potential benefits and obstacles incorrectly. We exaggerate the gains and minimize the opportunities we'd find outside our relationship. Divorce may be the right decision, but there will be real losses, too.

Make the best educated guess and then weigh the possible loss against the price for remaining in a gaslighting relationship, especially one that leaves you depressed and joyless.

2. **Fear of Abandonment and Being Alone**—Many of us have a general fear of abandonment. The idea of leaving or diminishing a relationship may trigger profound feelings of aloneness. For some, our identity is organized around being in a relationship or having

a particular job. If we face our fears and choose wisely, we may be grateful for the decision that preserved our integrity.

3. **Fear of Humiliation**—For many it feels like a profound humiliation to admit that things have turned out so badly. Leaving a relationship seems like an admission of failure. Rather than look realistically at our gaslighters, we'd rather keep our heads down and keep trying. Unfortunately, we can't get very far by avoiding the truth. You'll never find a way to become happier—with or without the relationship—by ignoring the truth. The price of humiliation is a small price to pay for freeing yourself from misery.

4. **Fear of Feeling Shame**—For some, the shame of violating your own integrity or other values keeps you trying to "right" the relationship and climb out of the shame rather than getting out of the relationship. For some, the recognition that you have allowed your life to go so far off track, or that you have created relational conditions only to satisfy the gaslighter, is not something you can allow yourself to face—so you keep going. Sometimes for years.

5. **The Power of Fantasy**—We see our gaslighter as our soul mate, the person we can't live without, and the great love of our life. For all of us, fantasy plays a powerful role in gaslighting relationships, though we may not recognize it.

Fantasies, Not Facts

- "I am so good and powerful that I can make him nicer by loving him."
- "It started so well. I can't believe we can't get back there."
- "He's my soul mate. No one has ever made me feel the way he does."
- "I think about him all the time. I love him so much. I can't imagine life without him."
- "She's my best friend. She's always been my best friend. She's always been there."
- "She knows me so well. Nobody knows me the way she does."
- "She can see right through me. I need someone like that in my life."
- "I have so many wonderful memories of her. We've been through so much together."
- "This is the best job I ever had. I owe this man everything. I can't let him down."
- "I'll never get another job like this one."
- "No one will ever take a chance on me the way he did."
- "He's so talented and he's really going places. I don't want to lose my chance to benefit."

- "She's my mother. She'd do anything for me. How can I let her down?"
- "I've always been able to depend on my father. Even if he does yell at me, he always comes through for me in the end."
- "My sister is like my best friend. Even if we fight all the time, I know I can count on her."
- "I've always looked up to my big brother. Even when he seems to belittle me, I know he's really on my side."

Making It Personal—In Your Own Words

What is your fantasy?

_____

_____

_____

_____

6. **Exhaustion and Depletion**—When you are exhausted or depleted, you don't think as clearly and don't make the best decisions. It's hard to focus—either on your own feelings (which are numbed anyway) or on what others are telling you about your relationship.

What are your personal insights? Do any of these reasons feel familiar?

_____

_____

_____

Those of us who stay in gaslighting relationships have decided (usually unconsciously) that we need to be able to tolerate anything and that we have the power to fix anything. No matter how badly we are treated, we _could or should_ be loving enough to make things work. We try to see ourselves as strong, tolerant, understanding, and forgiving—anything to make our partner's failings irrelevant.

Beneath these hopeful ideas lies a pool of sorrow, anger, and fear—the feelings of a child who can't depend upon having a loving and powerful adult to take care of them. We all need recognition, admiration, and love from others . . . and authentic connection. When we choose someone to fulfill those childhood wishes, we are very drawn to them.

But those who are prone to gaslighting are more than drawn; we are compelled by three fantasies.

1. Our partner (gaslighter) will be our sole source of nurturing.
2. We can change them by sheer force of our tolerance, love, and example.
3. We are strong enough (or forgiving or nurturing enough) to transcend any unwanted behavior.

Instead of their bad behavior making us like them less and feel less connected, it offers yet another chance to prove how strong we are. But we need to be wise and humble enough to gather our strength at our lowest point, and to be our own parent and take care of ourselves. *Let's take a look at what that means . . .*

Making It Personal—What if your love no longer felt like a thrilling, dangerous adventure, but instead simply brought a comforting, secure, and enjoyable companionship? How would you feel? _____

_____

_____

UNDERSTANDING THE BEHAVIOR

Erasing Yourself to Please Another

Healthy development as a child allows you to develop a true sense of self while maintaining a secure and positive attachment to your caregiver.

However, if you were unable to develop an authentic sense of self as a child, you may have learned that you must essentially **erase yourself** or risk losing the ties to those you were dependent on.

This accommodation typically manifests in one of three ways.

1. You do not want to lose the connection to your caregiver. Instead, you learn to sacrifice parts of yourself to preserve the essential emotional connection.

2. Alternatively, you may begin to isolate from your caregiver to be true to your authentic experience and inner truth.

3. Or you may move back and forth between these behaviors, pretending to be the good child at times and at other times defiantly clinging to your own inner experience (i.e., needs, wants, feelings, etc.).

If you grew up being overly accommodating, you may have found yourself in a no-win situation: Either you sacrificed key parts of your identity or you risked losing the close ties to your parents, who are so important to you.

Taking It Deeper—The "Why"

Pathological Accommodation (Insecure Attachment into Adulthood)—Because humans are highly social beings—the most social in the animal world—we naturally seek a secure attachment to our caregivers. This is understandable because of the extended time we are dependent on them. This attachment imperative unfolds for all of us as an unconscious developmental process, that is, we must learn how to create and optimize a secure attachment.

Depending on the unique relational dynamics between ourselves and our caregivers, we may grow up believing that maintaining a secure attachment requires the denial of our personal reality, including our longings, feelings, and opinions. This is seen as an **accommodation** attachment strategy. In other words, we unconsciously adopt the views and feelings of another at the expense of our own inner experience.

We may come to see this accommodation as our special strength in navigating relationships. However, successful mastery of this strategy essentially means that we have become very skilled at putting the other's needs before our own. Dr. Bernard Brandshaft saw **giving up one's authentic self to please and stay connected to the other as a form of "pathological accommodation."**

It's pathological because, once learned, this behavior is likely to continue into adult life and become habitual (unconscious) unless a conscious effort is made to change it.

Finding Yourself—Take a Deeper Dive ... How Do You Erase Yourself?

If you take a moment to breathe and reflect, do you recognize any behavior in yourself that you suspect could be pathological accommodation?

_____

_____

Please describe it.

_____

_____

Do you know when it began?

_____

_____

How would you describe this ability? Is it a special skill? A survival mechanism? Something else?

_____

_____

Are You Gaslighting Yourself?

Self-Sabotage

You question yourself as well as your goals and aspirations. Your self-confidence is undermined because you believe you are undeserving, or incapable, of attaining your desires.

When you gaslight yourself, you focus first on the negatives in your life, but at the same time, you think things could always be worse or that you're making it all up. Self-gaslighting prevents you from pursuing positive change. After all, if you don't believe your situation is that bad, you won't take action to change it.

Telltale Signs That You Are Gaslighting Yourself

- You minimize your own feelings.
- You constantly blame yourself.
- You doubt yourself.
- You are your own worst critic.
- You question yourself, including your memory.

This may sound familiar since it is similar to how you feel if you are being gaslighted by someone else. However, in this case *you* are the perpetrator. You are convincing yourself that something is true when it isn't. You embrace your doubts and are blind to your strengths and potential.

To challenge this habitual way of thinking, start by paying attention to how you talk to yourself about you and then practice shifting from negative self talk (trash self talk) to positive self talk.

Trash Self-Talk: Can You Get in Touch with Some of Your Trash Self-Talk?

What do you tell yourself repeatedly about your "deficits"? *For example: "I'm not good with names. I never remember anyone's name and feel embarrassed when I can't address them respectfully. I might actually avoid them."*

_____

_____

_____

Do you remember when you first started believing this? What were the circumstances? Who was present (caregiver/significant other)? Did they criticize, mock, or gaslight you and reinforce this negative belief about yourself?

_____

_____

If you had a friend who is feeling the same way about themselves, what would you say? Can you embrace this loving support for yourself?

_____

_____

_____

In the depth of winter, I finally learned that
within me there lay an invincible summer.

—Albert Camus

VISUALIZATION: CREATING A NEW WORLD

1. Imagine that you live in a beautiful house, surrounded by a beautiful fence. Take a moment to picture this house—its setting, its rooms, its furnishings. Take a moment to visualize the fence as well. What is it made of? How high is it? I want you to **imagine this fence as very strong**, so strong and so high that no one can breach it.

2. Find the doorway or gate in the fence through which welcome guests may enter. Realize that **you are the sole gatekeeper; you have complete power over who enters and who does not**. You may invite in whomever you choose. Likewise, you can keep out whomever you want, too, without even giving a reason. Take a moment to **feel what that power would be like**. Allow the faces of those you'd let in float into your mind. Then picture the people you'd want to keep out. Feel your power as the gatekeeper of your house.

3. Imagine you've decided that only people who truly care for you, who speak to you with kindness and consider your feelings with regard, can come in. **If anyone enters and then abuses you or twists your reality in any way, they must leave and can't come back** until they are prepared to treat you the way you want to be treated. You may also get tired of the people who alternate between dismissing you and treating you with regard, so perhaps you will decide not to let them in no matter how kind they're being!

4.   Continue to visualize your house, your walls, and your gate for five to ten minutes. Allow yourself to **see who wants to come in** and **whom you want to let in. Picture what happens as you decide yes or no**. See the responses of the people you've rejected or accepted and experience your response to their responses.

5.   Afterward, if you like, write about what you learned from this experience or talk about it with a friend. Remember, **you can use your gated house as a sanctuary** that will be there for you **any time** you want it.

Nowhere can man find a quieter or
more untroubled retreat than in his own soul.

—Marcus Aurelius

Reflection

Now, let's reflect on your visualization. What was it like for you to do that?

_____

_____

_____

What did you learn from this experience?

_____

_____

_____

Are you surprised by who you let into your beautiful house and who you didn't?

_____

_____

_____

_____

How did you feel having so much control over your choices? Was it a pleasure, a relief, or was it very difficult? Were you surprised by anything?

_____

_____

_____

Was it surprisingly difficult? If so, explore why . . .

_____

_____

_____

Draw Your World

Focus your attention on the people in your life and reflect for a moment as you draw your world. This can provide a surprising layer of clarity and objectivity to the relationships surrounding you.

The drawing will be a **sociogram**, a wonderful visual tool used to capture, in a picture, relationships within a group at a given point in time. In this case, you are drawing your personal "group" of relationships (e.g., family, friends, work colleagues).

By placing relationships in visual proximity to you, based on emotional closeness and importance in your life, and then stepping back to take a look, you will gather information about your interpersonal space, energetic ties, and feelings for each person.

Let's get ready to create your personal sociogram. I'll walk you through the steps.

- ✔ You can use color, size, and distance, and embellish your circles and lines any way you want to reflect *how this relationship really makes you feel* and the *frequency or intensity of interactions.*
- ✔ First, draw yourself in the middle of the page.
- ✔ Then begin drawing circles (with names representing relationships in your life) as they spontaneously come to mind. *(Don't overthink this; it's a bit like automatic writing.)*

Here's an example:

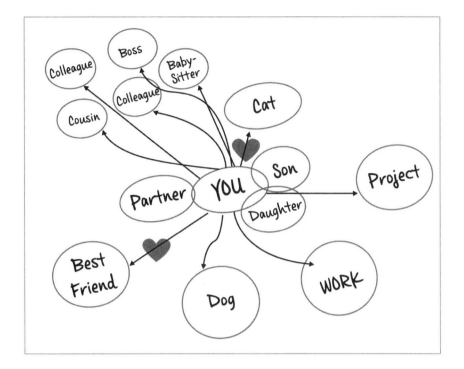

✔ Draw these circles in proximity to you based on how close you feel or how important they are to you. Sometimes you don't feel positively about all the people who are important to you—for example, your boss or your aunt—but because they are big in your life, they are big on the page.

✔ Now draw an expressive and directional line between you and them.

✔ Continue to build until you feel satisfied, allowing the drawing to take on a life of its own.

✔ Now take a moment and look at your drawing. Observe where you placed your relationships in proximity to you and how you feel about them.

✔ Then imagine that you move higher to observe it from your hot-air balloon. Allow memories to surface of specific interactions and feelings that prompted you to draw a particular circle-relationship exactly where you put it.

Your Personal Sociogram

Use this page to draw your personal sociogram, and remember you don't have to share it with anyone unless you want to.

In Your Own Words—Take a moment to step back and reflect on the world of relationships you have drawn around yourself. When you are in touch with your feelings, write your responses to the following questions as honestly as you can. If you want to, you can add your own question-and-answer section.

What is your first feeling-response? Look at the sociogram you created: Do you feel happy, satisfied, disappointed, sad, or something else?

_____

_____

_____

Does anything surprise you about the drawing?

_____

_____

_____

Is there anything you'd like to change? If so, what?

_____

_____

_____

Look at each individual relationship and consider how you feel about each person you have drawn a circle for. Who would you like to bring closer? Who would you like to let go of or take a step back from?

_____

_____

_____

6

Turning Off the Gas

You now understand what traps you in the Gaslight Tango. You've seen how difficult the three stages of gaslighting can be, and you have completed several exercises designed to help you reflect on how you got here and the pathways to a better life. It's time to turn off the gas!

In this chapter, we'll look closely at several techniques for setting limits, **connecting to the values you hold dear,** and **strengthening your internal core of self-respect**—the first steps to turning off the gas.

You can't turn off the gas until you've fully mobilized yourself to take action. Doing so will prepare you for any barriers or resistance you may encounter, both from your **gaslighter** and from **yourself**. You need to be willing to leave if your gaslighter continually punishes you for having your own thoughts.

In this chapter, we will explore:

- **Mobilizing Yourself to Act**—A six-point plan
- **Turning Off the Gas**—Five suggestions

Unexpected "Wow" Moments

A place to keep your spontaneous insights...

_____

_____

_____

_____

_____

Making the Decision to Turn Off the Gas

You need to be willing to leave if things don't change, as hard as it may be to contemplate. However, there may also be situations where you don't have to leave.

- Gaslighting creeps into a relationship gradually. In some situations, it can be rooted out again.
- A person usually resorts to gaslighting when they feel especially insecure. The issue can be solved by refusing to engage and avoiding gaslight triggers (phrases, actions, or situations).
- If you are both willing to admit there's a problem, a good couple's counselor might be able to help. Alternatively, your own awareness may be enough to shift the dynamic.
- You may be able to reduce your involvement without cutting off all contact. It is helpful to know this for relationships with family members.

You must be willing to leave, or the process won't work. And remember, it is human nature to slip back into old ways; people don't change all at once.

- *Caution!* Making changes may increase the gaslighting. Your gaslighter may step up the gaslighting, invoking more severe versions of their Emotional Apocalypse from yelling to screaming, from occasional criticism to constant criticism, from periodic freeze-outs to days of silence.
- You may be overcome with the Urge to Merge or be overwhelmed with longing for your gaslighter's approval. You might be tempted to forget the bad times and only remember the good ones.

Telltale Sign—Do any of these situations feel familiar? Describe your personal experience, what happens between the two of you, and your thoughts.

_____

_____

_____

_____

_____

_____

The only thing that will help your relationship change is your deep commitment to having a life you want—a life that is gaslight-free. Both you and your partner need to know that you will not stay in a relationship where you're not being treated with respect and where you're punished for having your own point of view.

Changing your own behavior is an extraordinary achievement that will repay you for the rest of your life. Just remember that the process of turning off the gas and mobilizing yourself to do so may take a long time. You will have bad days as well as good ones. Some days, you will feel yourself slipping backward; other days you will know that you've almost arrived. Keep breathing, be compassionate toward yourself, and stay close to the people you love and trust. As long as you're committed, you will get there in the end.

Things You Can Do to Encourage Your Resolve

- Commit to talking with trusted friends or loved ones once a day, or a therapist at least once a week, to keep your perspective.

- Write down your last three conversations with your gaslighter and edit them, reminding yourself how you would like to handle situations such as these in the future.

- Remember the last time you felt joyful. Write a description or create or find a picture that evokes that time. Post it where you can see it every day to remind yourself of what you want your new life to be like.

Encourage Yourself—As you read through the six suggestions for empowering your-self to act, remember that this is a journey that may involve many roads. Try these ideas if they feel right and in the order that works for you. You may even find yourself doing more than one step at a time.

You may not feel good about this process right away. Certainly, it might not feel com-fortable. As you start to see how things could be different, you may get in touch with levels of anger and despair that you didn't even know you were feeling.

Exploring these questions will take you into your own experience and memories. You may find it takes you away from the intellectual exercise of learning about gaslighting. But don't worry—I'll help you find your way back.

Our ambitions can only be limited by our doubts.

—Rajesh Khanna, Indian actor and politician

Preparing Yourself to Turn Off the Gas: A Six-Point Plan

1. Name your gaslighting dynamic.
2. Give yourself permission to make a sacrifice.
3. Check in with your feelings.
4. Get in touch with your values.
5. Empower yourself and surround yourself with love.
6. Take one step to improve your life. Then take another.

1. Name your gaslighting dynamic.

Reflection—This exercise is designed to help you find clarity.

a. What my *partner gaslighter* often does to gaslight me: _____

_____

_____

What I do as a gaslightee:

- My Behavior _____
- My Feelings _____
- My Thoughts _____

b. What my *friend gaslighter* often does to gaslight me: _____

_____

_____

What I do as a gaslightee:

- My Behavior _____
- My Feelings _____
- My Thoughts _____

c. What my *boss gaslighter* often does to gaslight me: _____

_____

_____

What I do as a gaslightee:

- My Behavior _____
- My Feelings _____
- My Thoughts _____

d. What my *family gaslighter* often does to gaslight me: _____

_____

_____

What I do as a gaslightee:

- My Behavior _____
- My Feelings _____
- My Thoughts _____

One of the most soul-destroying aspects of being treated badly is when we tell ourselves that we deserve it. Sometimes being compassionate toward ourselves is the hardest task of all. But that is often when change truly begins.

2. Give yourself permission to make a sacrifice.

Leaving your gaslighting relationship may cost you something. Thus, being willing to leave (even if you don't end up leaving) often means facing the prospect of tremendous grief and loss. The point is, you don't know what will happen. What you do know is that you're in a relationship that is undermining your spirit and sapping joy from your life. Your gaslighting relationship is unlikely to get better if you do nothing. The only hope for change is if you act differently. Yes, you may be risking something of great value if you do that.

Questions to Help You Take That Leap of Faith

• Did I make a decision today that made me feel good about myself? What was it?

_____

_____

_____

• Did I make a decision today that made me feel bad about myself? What was it?

_____

_____

_____

• Am I living a life of integrity in alignment with my values?

_____

_____

_____

• If not, what must I do to bring my life into alignment with my values?

_____

_____

_____

• What is my vision of the best life I'm capable of?

_____

_____

_____

• What can I do to achieve that vision?

_____

_____

_____

• What am I giving up if I leave the relationship (what will it cost me)?

_____

_____

_____

3. Give yourself permission to have your feelings.

Often, we disconnect from our feelings so that we can remain in our gaslighting relationships. To turn off the gas, we must turn on our feelings. To reconnect to your feelings, try the following exercise.

Awakening Your Feelings

(Jot down your answers in any form you like—sentences, brief notes, or anything else that works for you. You can also draw or diagram your answers.)

• Recall the last event that had an emotional impact on you. It could be as major as a loved one's illness or as minor as a disagreement with a bank teller. Describe the incident.

_____

_____

_____

• What did you feel?

_____

_____

_____

• What did you think?

_____

_____

_____

• What did you do?

_____

_____

_____

Just being able to speak your feelings helps you connect with them. So does expressing your feelings in different ways like writing or drawing. Try this exercise to help you clarify how you're feeling.

Reawakening Your Feelings

Step One

Label a blank page "My Point of View." Under that title, draw a picture or design that expresses how you feel about your situation or about a particular problem you've been having with your gaslighter. Label a second blank page "Their Point of View" and make a similar drawing showing the situation from their perspective.

Step Two

Sometimes it's important to give yourself time to sit with your feelings and see how they affect you. Put both pages away for twenty-four hours. When you look at them again, have another blank page ready. Write down whatever thoughts and feelings arise from this second viewing. Perhaps this new perspective on your feelings will help you discover an unexpected inner resolve to take action and stand up for yourself.

Clues That You May Be Burying Your Feelings

(Check the ones that feel familiar.)

- ☐ You feel "numb," flat, apathetic, or bored.
- ☐ You don't enjoy the things that used to give you pleasure.
- ☐ You feel sexually "dead." You don't enjoy sex, and attractive people don't turn you on—not even a little.
- ☐ Several times a month (or more), you experience physical symptoms such as migraines, stomach or intestinal ailments, backaches, colds or the flu, or accidental injuries.
- ☐ You have disturbing dreams.
- ☐ You find yourself reacting emotionally to things that you know don't mean much to you—crying at a TV commercial, for example, or losing your temper with a clerk.
- ☐ Your eating patterns change. Either you eat compulsively, or food doesn't interest you.

- [ ] Your sleeping patterns change. Either you're sleeping longer hours, or you're having difficulty falling asleep—or sometimes both.
- [ ] You feel tense and jumpy for no apparent reason.
- [ ] You feel exhausted or depleted for no apparent reason.

Telltale Sign—In Your Own Words . . .

Is there something you do or feel that is not on this list? What would you add? Please reflect on your personal experience, thoughts, and feelings and write down anything else you want to check.

_____

_____

_____

_____

4. Get in touch with your values.

In today's busy world, we rarely take the time to ask ourselves what our true core values are, what is most important to us, and what makes us feel joyful and fulfilled. Take some time now to reflect and list the values that are the most important for you in living a fulfilling, productive, compassionate, and loving life.

_____

_____

_____

_____

5. Empower yourself and surround yourself with love.

A gaslighting relationship often leaves us feeling helpless and incompetent, as though we can't do anything right. Beginning to see and own your strengths can be a critical part of making changes.

Empower Yourself By...

List your strengths and rely on them to help you cope:

_____

_____

_____

_____

Move from negative self-talk to positive self-talk:

_____

_____

_____

_____

Do things that help you regain your competence and confidence:

_____

_____

_____

_____

Avoid people who have negative opinions of you and who sap your energy:

_____

_____

_____

Surround yourself with people who see and support your strengths:

_____

_____

_____

_____

List Your Strengths—What about yourself are you proudest of? If you have a difficult time feeling pride, what about yourself makes you smile? Rely on your strengths to help you move through this difficult time.

_____

_____

_____

_____

_____

_____

_____

_____

Ask a friend to help you list your strengths.

_____

_____

_____

_____

What negative self-talk can you change to positive self-talk?

_____

_____

_____

_____

What things can you do that will make you feel competent?

_____

_____

_____

_____

_____

_____

List the people who sap your energy. Are there other people you would prefer to avoid?

_____

_____

_____

_____

List friends who celebrate your strengths. Are there other people you would like to surround yourself with?

_____

_____

_____

_____

_____

6. Take one step to improve your life. Then take another.

It's amazing how powerful it is to take an action—even a small one—that makes your life better. Even if your action seems to have nothing to do with your relationship, taking it will help you mobilize to turn off the gas.

The sense of empowerment from taking action can help move you to challenge your gaslighter. It may feel difficult to turn off the gas, because after weeks, months, or years of being gaslighted, you're no longer the same strong self you were when you entered your gaslighting relationship. Restoring that empowered self to take action is a powerful tool in your mobilization to turn off the gas.

If you have a great ambition, take as big a step as possible in the direction of fulfilling it. The step may only be a tiny one, but trust that it may be the largest one possible for now.

—Mildred McAfee, the first woman commissioned
as an officer in the U.S. Navy

UNDERSTANDING THE BEHAVIOR

The New You: Rewire Your Brain

We all have negative and counterproductive reactions, responses, and behaviors that we don't like about ourselves and may wish to change. Change implies personal growth, which is difficult because it involves breaking unconscious habits. It can be especially hard when it comes to relationships both with others and with ourselves, where we tend to react and respond without thinking. The more often these unconscious behaviors are repeated, the more they become ingrained.

Personal growth and change in relationships require us to become more fully aware of our feelings and how they inform our unconscious reactions and responses. We also need to discover that we have a choice as to how we feel, react, respond, and behave in the moment.

In fact, **practicing making different choices and doing these exercises will help rewire your brain** (that is, create new neural brain circuits). Every time you make a new choice it will become easier and easier to make it again as those neural circuits become stronger.

Taking It Deeper—The "Why"

The Neurobiology of Human Growth and Change

Thoughts and feelings inform our behavior, both consciously and unconsciously. Thoughts and feelings are mental representations that are created by synaptic firing patterns in the brain. The brain's physical processes create our experience of nonphysical mental representations of the mind (our thoughts and feelings). Thus, the mind is an emergent property of the physical activity of the brain. But these thoughts and feelings then directly influence our repeated patterns of reaction, responses, and behaviors. Here's how.

The habitual nature of this physical-mental process of mind and brain is explained by Hebb's axiom: "Neurons that wire together fire together." Psychologist Donald O. Hebb discovered that when neurons fire together, there is a physiological change that makes them want to fire together again. This phenomenon allows neurons to create complex circuitry that when activated produces the complex thoughts and feelings that inform human reactions, responses, and behaviors.

Thus, changing your behavior requires developing new synaptic firing patterns and neurocircuitry in the brain that will produce new thoughts, feelings, and behaviors in a given relational situation.

Neuroscientists refer to this process as neuroplasticity or rewiring your brain.

Finding Yourself—Take a Deeper Dive . . . How Are You Stuck?

Are you in touch with any of your automatic emotional reactions and responses? How would you describe them?

_____

_____

What triggers this response?

_____

_____

Do you feel capable of changing it?

_____

_____

Would you like to change your habitual reaction?

_____

_____

Do you believe that you have a choice?

_____

_____

Turning Off the Gas

Here are five shifts to try to alter the dynamic between you and your gaslighter.

Five Ways to Turn Off the Gas

1. Sort out truth from distortion.
2. Decide whether the conversation is really a power struggle. If it is, opt out.
3. Identify the triggers for both you and your gaslighter.
4. Focus on feelings instead of "right" and "wrong."
5. Remember that you can't control anyone's opinion—even if you're right!

1. Sort out truth from distortion.

Often, our gaslighters tell us their version of events, and we get completely thrown. There's just enough truth in their version to make us think that the whole package is true. Sorting out the truth from the distortion can be a helpful step in turning off the gas.

Pay close attention to what your gaslighter says and how the conversation flows. Write down, "I said, he said, I said, he said" to the best of your ability and see—in black and white—how your gaslighter distorts what has happened or pivots away from it, making their agenda the new and only topic to be discussed.

2. Decide whether the conversation is really a power struggle. If it is, opt out.

Gaslighting is so insidious that you don't always realize what the conversation is really about. A fight can continue for hours with the gaslighter becoming angrier and more intense, trying to prove they are right, and you becoming more and more desperate, trying to win them over. If you can't convince them, you may start to feel that their accusations are correct.

If you are not arguing about an actual incident, you can be sure you are enmeshed in a power struggle. The difference between a power struggle and a genuine conversation is this: **In a genuine conversation, both people are listening to and addressing each other's concerns,** even if they get emotional at times.

If you decide that a power struggle is going on, your first step in turning off the gas is to identify it and disengage. Otherwise, you're still dancing the Gaslight Tango.

Telltale Signs

(Check what feels familiar.)

You Know It's a Power Struggle If . . .

____ It includes a lot of insults.

____ You keep covering the same ground.

____ You are committed to being right or getting the other to agree with your point of view.

____ One or both of you bring in points that are way off topic.

_____ You've had the same argument several times before and have never really gotten anywhere.

_____ No matter what you say, the other person keeps having the same response.

_____ You feel as if the other person is simply in charge.

For things to say to opt out of the Right–Wrong Debate, see page 70. For ways to opt out while still expressing anger, see page 71. For ways to opt out using your own words, see page 102.

3. Identify the triggers for both you and your gaslighter.

Both you and your gaslighter are dancing the Gaslight Tango, and you both likely have triggers that start the dance. **Once you can identify these triggers, you will be more successful in avoiding them.** Triggers can range from topics like family and money to specific situations, language, or behaviors. Either of you might start the tango, depending on the situation. Try to approach this topic without shame or blame. Focus on identifying your mutual gaslight triggers so you both can start turning off the gas.

Think about _topics and situations_ that might trigger gaslighting.

_____

_____

_____

_____

Think about things _you say or do_ that might trigger their gaslighting.

_____

_____

_____

_____

Think about your gaslighter. Are there particular situations in which they're especially prone to gaslight you? Can you step back with compassion for yourself and observe your unwitting participation in the dynamic? When those situations arise, can you commit to being mindful and stepping away rather than participating in the Gaslight Tango?

Think about *power plays or manipulative actions* that may trigger their gaslighting.

_____

_____

_____

Think about ways you seek your gaslighter's *approval* and insist on their *reassurance.* *What is your habitual pattern?*

_____

_____

Alternate Responses to Avoid the Tango

- **Make a joke:** "Boy, if I didn't know I was the most beautiful woman in the world, I'd start to think I should worry."
- **Ask a question:** "Oh, you think I'm stupid? Wow, you're obviously seeing something I'm missing in this situation. Can you tell me more about what you're seeing?" Be aware that if you say this in a sarcastic tone, you are throwing fuel on the fire, but if you can ask sincerely, you may open up a response.
- **Identify the behavior:** "Last time you said that to me [or used that tone of voice], you were upset about having to go to your mother's for dinner. Is there something similar going on now?"
- **Express compassion:** "It looks like something is really upsetting you? Am I reading that correctly? Is there anything I can do to help?"
- **Opt out:** "I didn't mean to start an argument; let's take a pause."

Making It Personal—In Your Own Words…

What would you say to avoid the trigger?

_____

_____

_____

4. Focus on feelings instead of "right" and "wrong."

A gaslighter frequently makes accusations that ring true. Your gaslighter zeros in on these vulnerable moments or missteps, and you wince in recognition. To free yourself from this trap, stop worrying about which one of you is right and focus on your feelings.

- **If you're feeling genuine remorse,** apologize and do your best to make up.
- **If you are feeling angry because you are being unfairly criticized,** slow down your reaction and check: Take a deep breath and reference one of the alternate "opting-out" responses (pages 70, 71, and 102).
- **If you are feeling bewildered, attacked, devastated, or terrorized,** no matter what you did—even if you also feel regret—you are being gaslighted and you should disengage immediately.

5. Remember that you can't control anyone's opinion—even if you're right!

One of the biggest hooks in the gaslighting process is a desperate wish to get the other to agree that you are right. In reality, you are just as committed to controlling your gaslighter's thoughts as they are to controlling yours. They alone have the power over their own thoughts and will see things their way no matter what you do or say. As soon as you understand that it doesn't matter how right you are, the closer you will be to freedom.

> *Out beyond ideas of wrongdoing and*
> *rightdoing there is a field. I'll meet you there.*
>
> —Rumi

Practice Opting Out

Review the opting-out statements (page 102)—Pick the statements that fit your personality and which your gaslighter will most likely be able to hear. Edit them if needed or write your own.

_____

_____

_____

Role-play with a friend—Coach your friend on how to play your gaslighter, telling her what they are likely to say. Then play yourself and see what it feels like to use these new statements. Prepare by writing your dialogues here.

_____

_____

_____

Write your own script—Write out a conversation yourself. Imagine what your gaslighter might say and come up with your own responses. Practice saying them out loud.

_____

_____

_____

Focus on a few statements—Your goal is to opt out of the argument. Pick one or two helpful statements and either keep repeating them or stay silent. Your gaslighter is deeply committed to being right, so you aren't going to change their mind, but you may show them that their behavior has consequences.

_____

_____

_____

Choose your consequences—Decide ahead of time what consequences, if any, you will announce. Just make sure not to announce any consequence you aren't prepared to act on. Your goal isn't to threaten but to act in your best interest.

_____

_____

_____

Pick an exit strategy—If your gaslighter refuses to end the argument, end the conversation by hanging up, walking away, changing the subject, or even offering tea. Knowing how you will terminate the conversation will make you feel more empowered from the start.

_____

_____

_____

7

Should I Stay or Should I Go?

Choosing Your Next Step—Now that you have started to turn off the gas, you can expect some responses. You and your gaslighter may be finding new ways of being together, or maybe your gaslighter is absolutely refusing to change. Or perhaps you are still trying to sort out how you feel about possible next steps. You may have already decided what you want to do. If you haven't, in this chapter we are going to take a deep dive into **how to decide whether to go or stay**.

Unexpected "Wow" Moments

A place to keep your spontaneous insights . . .

_____

_____

_____

_____

_____

Taking Time for a Decision

If you're committed to freeing yourself from gaslighting, there will come a time when you need to decide whether you want to stay in the relationship or let it go. Remember, the only way to free yourself from gaslighting is to be *willing* to leave. After you try on some strategies and take the time you need, you face the decision to actually leave or not. You may even feel you don't have a choice; if you want to preserve your sense of self, the relationship has to end.

Alternately, you may feel you can make this relationship work or decide that there are good reasons for staying despite the pain and frustration. The good feelings you have for your gaslighter are not necessarily illusions. Your gaslighter may have behaved in abusive, problematic ways but may have also given you love, affection, attention, advice, adventure, or security. They may be someone who has qualities you admire, or someone who simply moves you for no reason you can name.

The realization or discovery that you have been abused, manipulated, and badly treated leads to emotional reactions. Allow all feelings—you likely will have many. Part of your *frustration* may be with yourself. How could you have been so blind? How could you have let yourself be treated so badly? You may feel a complicated mixture of *shame, resentment, anger,* and *sorrow* as you start to look more closely at your gaslighter and at your part in the gaslighting relationship. These feelings are important to notice and feel. Be curious and avoid judging yourself. Allowing the feelings will help you know yourself more deeply, understand what happened, and point you in a direction forward.

Four Questions to Ask About Staying or Going

1. ____ Can I act differently with this person?
2. ____ Are they capable of acting differently with me?
3. ____ Am I willing to do the work it might take to change our dynamic?
4. ____ Realistically, if I give it my best effort, will I be happy with our relationship?

1. Can I act differently with this person?

Turning off the gas requires that you detach from your gaslighter, opt out of the conversation, or walk out of the room. It means you must resist the Urge to Merge. Here are some questions to ask yourself about how much you're willing to change.

When they begin gaslighting me, can I opt out of the conversation or will I need to prove to them I'm right? Will I keep arguing with them in my head, even if I don't say anything out loud?

_____

_____

If my partner's gaslighting makes me feel anxious about myself or the relationship, will I need to turn to them for reassurance? Can I imagine finding some way of calming myself down that doesn't depend on them?

_____

_____

If I say I'm going to do something—such as leave the room when they yell or leave the restaurant if they are more than twenty minutes late—will I be able to stick to what I've said?

_____

_____

Can I act differently with this person? *(Reflecting on what you have learned about yourself and given your previous answers, how would you answer this question now?)*

_____

_____

2. Are they capable of acting differently with me?

A person turns to gaslighting when they feel off-balance psychologically: Maybe they're threatened, stressed, or envious. They respond by "righting themself"—using gaslighting to find inner stability and proving that they are okay and/or right. This stabilization is a way for them to feel powerful and strong in the world. And it's how they hold on to their sense of who they are. Some people are deeply committed to gaslighting due to profound insecurities in their sense of self. Others may gaslight occasionally in response to stresses within or outside the relationship, or just because they know it works. If they're irredeemable, they might also find pleasure in it.

How committed are they to gaslighting?

_____

_____

Suggestion Box

If you're not sure, try the following exercise.

- For one week, make every effort to turn off the gas. Don't accept a single invitation to join the Gaslight Tango or miss one opportunity to step away. Avoid all temptations to control, explain, analyze, fantasize, or negotiate. At some point they will try to draw you in, but see what happens if you refuse.

- Keep a daily journal of your experience and observations.

- At the end of the week, without looking at your journal, assess how you feel and how you think the week went. Do you think you were able to turn off the gas? If not, why not?

- Spend some time reviewing your journal and the feelings that come up while you read it. Does your journal reflect your memory of the week?

How Capable Is My Gaslighter of Connecting Deeply to Me?

Do they…

____Seem capable of understanding and respecting your point of view?

____At least occasionally tune in to your feelings and needs?

____At least occasionally put your feelings and needs ahead of their own?

____Feel remorse about the times they have hurt you—in a way that leads them to acknowledge your feelings, apologize, and to change their behavior?

____Express and show interest in changing for their own reasons? Or is it simply to please you or prove what a good person they are?

Are they capable of acting differently with me? (*Reflect on what you have learned about your gaslighter.*)

_____

_____

3. Am I willing to do the work it might take to change our dynamic?

It is difficult for couples to break free from a gaslighting dynamic together. It can become a vicious cycle in which insistent—sometimes aggressive—behavior provokes your defensive reaction, which in turn may trigger even more insistence or greater aggression from the other.

Gaslighting usually involves two people who both have a low tolerance for disagreement or conflict. Is this you? Your gaslighter can't stand it when you don't see the world their way. They need to convince you they're right, and you can't bear that they think so badly of you. Each of you brings an extra **intensity of need** to the relationship, and this intensity tends to set off another round of the Gaslight Tango.

Ask Yourself—What do you really need/want in this relationship?

_____

_____

Ask Them—What do they really need/want in this relationship?

_____

_____

Bringing Yourself into Focus—Ask yourself which statements **feel familiar,** and which statements **feel unfamiliar.**

You Might Trigger an Escalation in Gaslighting by . . .

Expecting to be put down

____ "I know I'm stupid."

____ "Please forgive me—you know I can be really absorbed."

____ "I can't believe how selfish I've been."

Begging for reassurance

____ "Even though I'm still a mess, you still love me, don't you?"

____ "I just get so lonely, honey. Can't you see how much I need you?"

Assuming they'll treat you badly

____ "Don't fly off the handle again."

____ "I know you'll think I'm stupid, but I can't help it, okay?"

In Your Own Words—What might you say that could trigger an escalation?

_____

_____

Here are some questions you can ask yourself as you decide whether the two of you can change your dynamic and live with more integrity.

Do I have the social support I need? *(Gaslighting challenges our ability to distinguish truth from distortion. It's difficult to challenge a gaslighter without a support system to help maintain your own sense of what's really going on.)*

_____

_____

Do I have the discipline to insist on my limits? *(You can't control your gaslighter, but you can control your own responses. You'll need to stick to whatever limits you set, no matter how painful that sometimes feels.)*

_____

_____

Do I have the discipline, energy, and courage to say, "Stop it"? *(This kind of change takes deep, concerted effort and energy. Are you willing to put this kind of work into saving your relationship, knowing it might not pay off?)*

_____

_____

Am I willing to make sacrifices? *(You may feel as though you are giving up much of what made your relationship pleasurable or worthwhile and that your efforts to save your relationship are in fact destroying it.)*

_____

_____

Am I willing to do the work it might take to change our dynamic? Realistically, if I give it my best effort, will I be happy in this relationship? *(Sum up what you've learned about the big questions.)*

_____

_____

This final question is the one that will really tell you what you want to do. Looking realistically at who you are, who your gaslighter is, and what you'll have to do to change your dynamic, **is it worth it to you?**

_____

_____

As you look at your responses, what is your immediate reaction?
*Can you hear yourself saying **Stay** or **Go**? Check in with your Flight Attendants.*

Making It Personal—Flight Attendants Who Might Signal Danger

- Does your stomach clench in protest? Y____ N____

- Do your friends raise their eyebrows and look away? Y____ N____

- Yes or no, if you imagine leaving do you feel dread ____ or does your anxiety lessen?____

In your own words . . . What are your Flight Attendants telling you?

_____

_____

_____

For a longer list of Flight Attendants, turn to page 52.

Reasons My Patients Have Given for Staying

1. ___ "I really enjoy the conversations I have with my partner."
2. ___ "I have never talked so deeply with anyone."
3. ___ "My partner is brilliant—I learn so much from him."
4. ___ "He is my soul mate."
5. ___ "I do love her, and our life together works."
6. ___ "If there's any way to make this relationship work, I owe it to my kids to try."
7. ___ "I hadn't realized how much I was participating in the problem. Let's see what happens when I shift my own behavior."
8. ___ "We have a long history together."
9. ___ "I admire my friend—she has a unique perspective—and I don't want to give up hearing her take on things."

10. ___ "I'm willing to see my mother less often, but I would never want to totally cut her out of my life."

11. ___ "I want my kids to know their relatives, and I'm willing to put up with a lot of unpleasantness to make that happen."

12. ___ "This job is probably good for another two years. After that, I'm moving on anyway."

13. ___ "My boss gave me a foot in the door when no one else would. I owe it to him to keep trying to make it work from my end."

14. ___ "I think I can still learn more from this work situation, so I'm going to grit my teeth and find a way to make it work."

15. ___ "I am actually so sensitive . . . I like the work here and think I do make a big deal about things, so maybe I can just ignore his criticism and put-downs."

Making It Personal—In Your Own Words . . .

What reason for staying would you add that may be more personal?

_____

_____

_____

_____

Reasons My Patients Have Given for Leaving

1. ___ "I never want to be in a relationship where I can't be proud and comfortable telling people how my partner talks to me and what he does."

2. ___ "Being in a relationship is supposed to make your life bigger and richer, and this one has made my life smaller and poorer. Even if that's my own responsibility, I'm still tired of it."

3. ___ "I don't want my children to grow up thinking that *this* is what a marriage is."

4. ___ "I don't think my friends would recognize me anymore."

5. ___ "When I think about him, I'm always anxious."

6. ___ "I don't like to be called names. Period."

7. ___ "I'm tired of feeling bad all the time."

8. ___ "I just don't want to feel this way anymore."

9. ___ "I cried all last night. Enough is enough."

10. ___ "I'm sick of thinking about this relationship. It's all I ever think about anymore!"

11. ___ "I am not living in line with my values."

12. ___ "If a friend's relationship sounded and looked like mine, I would advise them to get out."

13. ___ "It's as if a switch went off. I just can't do it anymore."

14. ___ "I shudder when I think I am a role model for my daughters."

15. ___ "I just want a peaceful, drama-free life."

Making It Personal—In Your Own Words . . .

What reason for leaving would you add that may be more personal?

_____

_____

_____

_____

_____

_____

Gap Exercise

What is the gap between your relationship now and what you want it to be?

_____

_____

"Where is my relationship now?"

_____

_____

"Where would I like my relationship to be?"

_____

_____

"What are the steps that I am going to take to get to where I would like it to be?"

_____

_____

Identify Your Barriers

What is your initial reaction when I talk about "going" or "staying"?

_____

_____

"What are the barriers keeping me from moving forward?"

_____

_____

"What are the barriers inside of me?" *For example: "I don't want to think about it so concretely."*

_____

_____

"What are the barriers outside of me?" *For example: "I don't want to bring it up because it will devastate my partner."*

_____

_____

"What are the steps I am going to take to address those barriers? How realistic is my plan?"

_____

_____

Pause and breathe—After completing these exercises, you might want to put the book down for a minute and give yourself a big dose of compassion. It's hard work to face your feelings. It's hard work to think about possibly making a move that will cause upheaval in your life, even if it's for a better life. Try focusing on your breath and performing a lovingkindness meditation. Or, if you prefer, think about a kindness you can give yourself in self-talk—perhaps in line with your values—like this:

Breathe in. "I want a relationship with lovingkindness and respect." Breathe out. Breathe in. "I will be with someone who treats me that way." Breathe out.

When you are ready to keep exploring, gently move on to the following exercise.

Visualize Your Relationship

This exercise will help you better understand your relationship so that you have a clearer sense of what decisions you want to make. If you can visualize exactly what is going on with your relationship, you can decide whether to stay, to leave, or to start taking the actions that are part of turning off the gas.

In order to make those decisions, you have to know how your relationship makes you feel. **Visualizing your current relationship** will help you with this.

1.   If there are problems in your relationship, **visualizing your past relationship** will make it clear to you how serious the problems are. If your relationship was once good and has since changed, you can decide whether it's realistic to recover the good elements while changing the bad ones. If you discover that your relationship has always upset you or frustrated you or left you feeling lonely, you can decide whether it's realistic to expect it to get better.

2.   **Visualizing your future relationship** will help you get in touch with how you truly feel and what you genuinely think about the possibilities your relationship holds. Is there a real chance of making it good, or can you not even imagine being happy with your partner? Asking these questions will bring you closer to a decision about whether to stay or leave, as will **visualizing the future without your gaslighting relationship**. If you like that future better than the alternative, maybe it's time to leave.

3.   **Finally, evaluating your relationship can help you decide what you want to do.** Perhaps you need to choose between staying or leaving. Or perhaps you'd like to try turning off the gas. Perhaps you'd like to give your relationship a time limit: If it hasn't improved by a certain point, then you'll reconsider and take new action. Whatever you choose, evaluating your relationship can help you come to a decision that is right for you.

Visualize Your Current Relationship

Close your eyes and allow yourself to think about your current relationship with your gaslighter.

- What images come to mind?
- What physical sensations do you notice?
- What emotions do you feel?
- How do you see yourself in this picture? What are your facial expressions? What is your body language? What are you doing or saying?
- How do you see your gaslighter in this picture? What are their facial expressions? What is their body language? What are they doing or saying?

Be mindful not to censor or judge any of the images, thoughts, or feelings that come to mind. Just allow your mind to drift where it will and then notice where it takes you.

When you've finished, open your eyes and complete each of the following sentences. Write as much or as little as you like. If you prefer, you can draw a picture or create an image that expresses your response.

The thing I like most about my gaslighter is _____
_____
_____

The thing I like least about my gaslighter is _____
_____
_____

Qualities I value in my gaslighter are_____
_____
_____

Qualities I value in myself when I am with my gaslighter are _____
_____
_____

When I'm frustrated with my gaslighter, I wish I could change _____
_____
_____

When I see us together, I'm most struck by _____
_____
_____

My Flight Attendants are telling me _____
_____
_____

As I write these answers, I feel _____
_____
_____

Right now, my body feels _____
_____
_____

How was that exercise for you? As always, go at your own speed. After a few minutes of thinking and writing about painful memories, take a minute to look into your future, where you will take what you learn from this relationship to brighten all that comes after. Each relationship gives us gifts—the gifts of learning about yourself in a new way. This is true even when the relationship is challenging. Even when you have crawled your way out. Even in gaslighting. You have the chance to rewrite your narrative, however painful, with an eye toward the lessons you are taking with you.

Visualize Your Past Relationship

Now close your eyes and allow yourself to think about your past relationship with your gaslighter.

- What images come to mind?
- What physical sensations do you notice?
- What emotions do you feel?
- How do you see yourself in this picture? What are your facial expressions? What is your body language? What are you doing or saying?
- How do you see them in this picture? What are their facial expressions? What is their body language? What are they doing or saying?

Again, don't censor or judge any of the images, thoughts, or feelings that come to mind. Just allow your mind to drift where it will as you notice where it takes you.

When you've finished, open your eyes and complete each of the following sentences.
The thing I like most about our past relationship is _____

_____

The thing I like least about our past relationship is _____

_____

Something I'd like to recapture from that time is _____

_____

Something I never want to repeat again is _____

_____

When I look at my gaslighter back then, I see a person who _____

_____

When I look at myself back then, I see a person who _____

_____

When I see us together, I see a couple [pair of friends, set of colleagues, mother and daughter, etc.] who _____

_____

My Flight Attendants are telling me _____

_____

As I write these answers, I feel _____

_____

Right now, my body feels _____

_____

Visualize Your Future Relationship

Close your eyes and open your mind. Allow yourself to think about a possible future relationship with your gaslighter. Visualize the two of you together next month, next year, five years from now.

- What images appear?
- What physical sensations do you notice?
- What emotions do you feel?
- Is your gaslighter someone you'd like to be involved with as a partner, friend, employee, colleague, or family member?
- Most important, are you the person you'd most like to be? Are you on the way to reaching your full potential, fulfilling your dreams, savoring the joy in your life? Are you imagining a future full of possibility and excitement, or do you find yourself feeling dread, anxiety, or regret?

Again, don't censor or judge anything that comes to your mind. Just keep asking yourself to visualize the future and see what comes up.

When you've finished, open your eyes, take a few deep belly breaths, and complete each of the following sentences.

The thing I like most about the future I imagine is _____

_____

_____

_____

_____

Something that concerns me about the future I imagine is _____

_____

_____

The person I want to become is someone who _____
_____
_____

My future relationship will help me become that person by _____
_____
_____

My future relationship may prevent me from becoming that person by _____
_____
_____
_____

My Flight Attendants are telling me _____
_____
_____

As I write these answers, I feel _____
_____
_____
_____

Right now, my body feels _____
_____
_____

Visualize Your Future Without Your Gaslighting Relationship

For the last time, close your eyes and allow your mind to wander toward a possible future relationship without your gaslighter. Visualize yourself without this relationship (or with a far more limited version of it) next month, next year, five years from now.

- What images appear?
- What physical sensations do you notice?
- What emotions can you name?
- Who are the important people in this picture with you?
- What activities do you enjoy in your visualized future?
- How are you feeling—pleasant or unpleasant?
- What are you doing in your visualization?
- Most important, are you the person you'd most like to be?

Be mindful not to censor or judge. Just be curious and allow your possible future to unfold in your mind's eye without your gaslighting relationship as you know it now.

When you've finished, open your eyes and complete each of the following sentences. The thing I like most about the future I imagine is _____

_____

_____

Something that concerns me about the future I imagine is _____

_____

_____

The person I want to become is someone who _____

_____

_____

Not being in my gaslighting relationship (or being in a much more limited version of it) will help me become that person by _____

_____

_____

Not being in my gaslighting relationship may prevent me from becoming that person by

_____

_____

_____

My Flight Attendants are telling me _____

_____

_____

As I write these answers, I feel_____

_____

Right now, my body feels _____

_____

Revisit Your Relationship

Now that you've thought about the **past, present,** and **future** of your gaslighting relationship, I invite you to consider a high-level reckoning of how that relationship is working for you and how you imagine it might work in the future. Remember to breathe while doing these exercises. Grab that pen and paper, and complete the following sentences. Remember, you can write as much or as little as you like.

When I imagine describing my relationship with my Flight Attendants—my surest guides to what's going on—I hear myself saying _____

_____

_____

When I imagine my Flight Attendants witnessing my relationship, what they see is ____

_____

_____

I'm picturing a child, younger sibling, or some other child I'm close to, and imagining that child growing up and being in a relationship just like mine. When I imagine this, I feel

_____

_____

_____

Since I've been in this gaslighting relationship, I feel I've become more_____

_____

_____

Since I've been in this gaslighting relationship, I feel I've become less _____

_____

_____

When I think about how being in this relationship has affected me, I feel_____

_____

_____

*The capacity to witness what is happening inside us
with a nonjudging attention allows us to respond to life
from our full intelligence and heart.*

—Tara Brach, psychologist and Buddhist teacher

Please consider the following questions carefully and then answer them.
(You can use words, images, sentences, or symbols.) You can come back to this over the next several days as you think of more pros and cons.

I might want to keep this relationship because …

_____

_____

_____

I might want to let go of this relationship because …

_____

_____

_____

Finally, take a moment to tune into **you.** You may want to close your eyes or gaze softly downward. Start with a few deep belly breaths. Send compassion to yourself. This is hard work. You are worth it, but it is hard!

Then Ask Yourself …

Do I really want my gaslighter in my world?

Does your heart brighten at the thought? Perhaps you'll want to stay. If your heart sinks or your stomach clenches, or you begin to feel numb or exhausted, you may want to leave. If you really can't decide, consider a mini-separation. Some time apart may really clarify the issue for you—and give your gaslighter the space to consider if they want to work on the relationship.

Unexpected "Wow" Moments

A place to keep your spontaneous insights . . .

_____

_____

_____

_____

_____

Be a loner. That gives you time to wonder, to search for the truth. Have holy curiosity. Make your life worth living.

—Albert Einstein

8

Keeping Your Life Gaslight-Free

Now that you've decided to either leave your gaslighting relationship or stay, you have a new challenge: keeping your life gaslight-free. Whether you're trying to change a gaslighting relationship from within, limit one, or leave one, you've got some work ahead. I can support you by walking you through it.

You understand your own role in the Gaslight Tango, and you've found new ways to step away from it. You've learned how to turn off the gas and have even practiced it. And you've decided to either leave your gaslighting relationship, limit it significantly, or try changing it from within.

What's Next?

Step 1: Decide Your Objective
- Are you trying to change your relationship from within? _____
- Are you trying to limit the intimacy of your relationship? _____
- Are you committed to leaving the relationship altogether? _____

If You're Trying to Change a Gaslighting Relationship from Within

This could be the most challenging option of all. You and your gaslighter have established a powerful dynamic, and it will require a lot of work and commitment to change it.

> If you would like to **change, limit,** or **leave** a gaslighting relationship, please remember to be gentle and patient with yourself as you reflect on the following suggestions, the specifics of how they may relate to you personally, and how you can apply them in the most productive way possible.

Here's what you'll need to do to change a gaslighting relationship from within.

1. **Invoke your integrity mindset**—Remember: Your actions are in service of your values.

2. **Be committed**—The only way your gaslighting dynamic will change is if **you** commit to change. Your gaslighter must also be aware and willing to behave differently, but if you don't alter your behavior, it will be difficult to expect a shift in theirs. Each and every time you get into the tango, remember to invoke your integrity mindset.

3. **Be aware of your emotions**—Check in with your own feelings regularly. Notice your responses to your feelings, both emotional and behavioral. Try to determine when your anxiety, sadness, anger, or loneliness is just a transient feeling and doesn't reflect the everyday reality of your life. Spend time reflecting on what you typically do when you are anxious, angry, or sad, or anything else. Remember that there are no good or bad emotions. Give yourself permission to have all your feelings—the pleasant and the unpleasant. All emotions are important sources of information. It's important to listen to what your emotions are telling you. And remember that, while you can't control them, you always have a choice about what you do about them.

4. **Be honest**—Hold the long view. Try keeping a calendar for one month. Every night jot down a few words that sum up your experience of the day. At the end of the month, copy experiences into a chart with two columns: Pleasant and Unpleasant. What does the chart say about your overall "feeling" of the month?

5. **Be disciplined and skillful**—Identify and use your most helpful emotion regulation strategies when you are uncomfortable and when you feel tempted to break your promise to use every possible opportunity to behave differently. Take a look at the appendix for a list of immediate, short-term, and long-term emotional regulation strategies. Add your own to your repertoire.

6. **Be responsible**—I don't mean that the gaslightee should take responsibility for the gaslighter's behavior or for the outcome of the relationship. But you can take responsibility for your own part in the dynamic and decide what you want to do if you find yourself in a Gaslight Tango.

7. **Be compassionate**—Be compassionate toward yourself as well as your gaslighter. It may be difficult to realistically see their needs and vulnerability once the gaslighting starts, because their gaslighting behavior is indeed painful and distorted. But consider that they may also be suffering. They may have grown up in a home where they were gaslighted by someone and couldn't make it stop. Or they were gaslighted by friends and are still living out that dynamic. So now they don't understand why you have the power to make it stop. Allow yourself to be a vulnerable, needy, flawed human being. It's part of being human. Your compassion may not alter your decision to leave or stay, but it will alter the tone—likely for both of you—and alter the narrative you tell, now and in the future.

If you feel ready, I want to invite you to try the second part of the Metta Meditation. If you are not ready to do this, please don't be hard on yourself. You can simply remember it's here if you would like to use this in the future.

After sending lovingkindness to yourself, call to mind your gaslighter and (if you are ready) send lovingkindness to them. This doesn't mean you're forgetting about the gaslighting, and it doesn't mean you want to stay, but it does mean you recognize the humanity and frailty in all of us, and you are sending them compassion. And being compassionate is likely something that is an important part of how you want to show up in the world now and going forward.

Starting with giving compassion to yourself, then calling your gaslighter to mind, breathe in and out deeply. After silently repeating these words to yourself, go back to giving yourself compassion.

Metta Meditation

May **I** be happy of mind

May **I** be healthy of body

May **I** be free of suffering

May **I** have ease of well-being

May **they** be happy of mind

May **they** be healthy of body

May **they** be free of suffering

May **they** have ease of well-being

May **I** be happy of mind

May **I** be healthy of body

May **I** be free of suffering

May **I** have ease of well-being

If You're Trying to Limit a Gaslighting Relationship

You may decide that certain relationships can remain gaslight-free when you're more distant but will inevitably involve gaslighting once they become intimate.

If you want to limit a gaslighting relationship without breaking it off entirely, these are the steps I encourage you to take:

1. **Be analytical**—Make a list of all the situations or topics that potentially trigger gaslighting in your relationship. Think about the time of day (perhaps at night when you are both tired), day of the week (for some, Friday nights), or time of the year (birthdays or holidays) that have the potential to create the ripe conditions for gaslighting.

2. **Be specific**—Using your analysis, decide several specific ways and times you can set boundaries or create some distance. After you think about how to best protect yourself from gaslighting, list what kinds of contact will work. Do you want to limit particular types of conversation (e.g., avoid long conversations with a friend), or would you prefer to see this person only in large groups or in a one-on-one situation? Think clearly about any barriers to keeping your limits and address them specifically.

Finish every day and be done with it. You have done what you could. Some blunders and absurdities, no doubt have crept in. Forget them as soon as you can. Tomorrow is a new day; begin it well and serenely, with too much a spirit to be cumbered with your old nonsense.

—Ralph Waldo Emerson

3. **Be creative**—Before deciding that something can't be done, see if you can come up with a creative way to work around the problem rather than confront it head-on. Surprise yourself with an alternate way of setting your limits, for example, meeting at a café instead of at home, creating promise vouchers to hand out, and so on.

4. **Be kind and firm**—Remind yourself that you have the right to set any limit you want, and then, secure in that knowledge that you won't give in, maintain that limit as calmly and kindly as you can. Use your favorite emotion regulation strategies to prepare for conversations or, when conversations derail, to help stay calm.

5. **Be disciplined and skillful**—If you don't give a consistent, steady message about the limits you want to set, you can be sure that within a matter of weeks your relationship will be right back to where it was before. Think carefully about that message. Be mindful about what you need for yourself to help you deliver the same consistent message. Remember: "No" is a whole sentence.

6. **Be committed**—Remember, until your gaslighter understands and agrees to work on changing your dynamic, you need to invest extra energy into making sure you get what you want, knowing that you may face a certain amount of opposition. Being committed involves a commitment to yourself for self-care. If you need some time apart to rest and rejuvenate, take it. Be sure you are eating healthy, sleeping well, and moving your body every day. Self-care basics will help fortify you and set you up for the ongoing work of keeping your commitment to a gaslight-free life.

7. **Be compassionate**—Show compassion to your gaslighter and yourself. Neither of you has chosen to be in this difficult situation, both of you are suffering, and both of you will make mistakes. Try to view yourself with compassion, even as you proceed with the tough decisions that you may need to make.

If You're Trying to Leave a Gaslighting Relationship

You may have decided that the only way to avoid the gaslighting in your relationship is to end the relationship entirely.

If your decision is to end the relationship, these are the steps I encourage you to take.

1. **Be in the present**—It hurts to leave a relationship. Even leaving a relationship that's no longer making you happy is a loss. You need to give yourself permission to feel all your feelings—the painful ones too. Stay in the present with your emotions and be mindful that you don't need to project them into the future. The future is as mysterious and full

of possibilities as it always was. Focus on your life now, live one day at a time, and let the future take care of itself.

2. **Be receptive to help**—Allow yourself to reach out. Ask for support from others you trust. You don't need to do this alone. Social support can bring comfort and serenity and lead to the insight and connection you need. Call friends and loved ones, find a therapist, take yoga, or meditate. Reaching out and accepting help in a time of trouble makes us stronger and lets others know you trust them. Salute yourself, and then reach out for help.

3. **Be patient**—You've taken a huge step toward making the changes you seek. But you can be sure they won't all happen immediately. Have patience, even when you feel otherwise. Keep breathing and allow yourself a bit more time to complete the process you've begun.

4. **Be compassionate**—Showing compassion can be very healing to both you and your gaslighter. Accept that you've done the best you can and offer yourself the compassion you deserve.

A fire
grows
simply because the space is there,
with openings
in which the flame
that knows just how it wants to burn
can find its way.

—Judy Brown, *The Sea Accepts All Rivers*

Some Long-Term Suggestions for Keeping Your Life Gaslight-Free

- Listen to your inner voice (take the time to daydream, walk, reflect).

- Write in a journal.

- Keep talking to trusted friends.

- If you are tempted to engage in a gaslighting relationship, think about what a trusted mentor or role model might say to you.

- Ask yourself: Is this person good enough for my daughter/sister/mother?

- Practice positive self-talk. Tell yourself, truthfully, what's good and admirable about yourself.

- Nurture yourself by connecting with your spirit. Make time for prayer, meditation, or simple quiet time to reconnect to your deepest self.

- Live through your integrity mindset—recall your values and the ways you believe people ought to treat each other.

- Spend time with people who affirm your spirit.

- Believe that "No" is a whole sentence and use it more often.

- Do your best to get some form of fulfilling physical activity every day.

- Find an assertiveness class or leadership training workshop where you can sharpen your skills in effective communication, self-advocacy, and negotiation.

- Do only what you want to do. If you are ambivalent, say "No." You will feel the strength of your convictions.

Make use of the exercises in this book that strengthen and clarify your mind, emotions, and spirit. I invite you to evoke the image of the beautiful house surrounded by a fence (see page 122), given to me years ago by a friend and colleague, Dr. Frank Lachmann. This fence is constructed so that only you can open its gate for visitors. Practice letting in the people with whom you feel safe, loved, and respected, and keeping out the people with whom you feel uncomfortable, judged, and devalued. Do this whenever your commitment needs strengthening. Remember that you have *total* control over who comes into your "house," and resolve not to let anyone inside who doesn't feel right to you. Promise yourself that you won't have even a single conversation in this house that feels wrong.

Rewriting Your Responses

One important key to remaining gaslight-free is to not allow your self-worth to depend on someone else's approval. Developing a strong, clear sense of yourself and your worth is crucial to staying out of gaslighting relationships.

In Your Own Words—Freewrite About Your Self-Worth

Do you feel that you are a person worthy of love and respect?
____Y ____N

If you have allowed your gaslighter to answer that question for you, even for a minute, or for way too long, take your power back now. Create several phrases, on a separate sheet of paper, about your value as a human being and what you want and feel entitled to in your relationship going forward.

Once you have these phrases, you can call them to mind regularly. Deliberately choosing compassionate and loving phrases is the positive self-talk that will lift and brighten the way forward—the way you see and think about yourself.

Personal Reflections

What words or phrases stand out for you? Write them down.

_____

_____

_____

What about the reflections resonates with you?

_____

_____

_____

Where do your thoughts take you?

_____

_____

_____

Keep your reflections—and your integrity—in mind when you choose new relationships and professional challenges.

Considering the Future

To truly live a gaslight-free future, look more closely at the aspects of gaslighting that feel compelling and ask yourself what is drawing you in. Gaslighting often holds a powerful allure beyond the aspects we've already discussed. We often feel that our gaslighting relationships offer us the promise of something more intense, more glamorous, and more special than other connections. The drama of the relationship can be part of its charm.

Many of us come to relationships with a hidden "extra" wish. We want the relationship to bring love and joy to the present, but we also want a way to repair the past. *They're the one who will make us whole, recuse us from loneliness, assure us that someone really does understand. We may also love the possibility that we can do the same for them.*

As you look toward the future and think about keeping your life gaslight-free, consider whether this extra thrill of the "electric and frantic" back-and-forth is really something you feel prepared to give up. Think deeply about what it could mean to you to create self-protective boundaries.

Accept that there will be some loss and maybe grief after a gaslighting relationship is over, alongside the relief and freedom in letting go. Your integrity is worth it. You are deserving of a safe, loving, and respectful partnership.

Keeping Things in Perspective

How do you distinguish between **ordinary imperfections** and **serious flaws**?

1. On balance . . .
    - Do you feel heard, appreciated, effective within the relationship? **Y / N**
    - Do you feel you're getting what you want? **Y / N**
2. Look to your Flight Attendants . . .
    - When you think about your relationship, do you feel joy, pleasure, and satisfaction? **Y / N**
    - Or do you feel anxiety, trepidation, and uncertainty? **Y / N**

As we go beyond the *should*s and *shouldn't*s, let's reflect on where we are and where we would like to be.

Summation Exercise

"Where am I now?"

_____

_____

_____

_____

"Where would I like to be?"

_____

_____

_____

_____

"What are the steps that I am going to take to get to where I would like to be?"

_____

_____

_____

_____

"What are the barriers keeping me from moving forward?"

_____

_____

_____

"What are the steps I am going to take to address those barriers?"

_____

_____

_____

Living with Integrity: Be Your Best Self

Part of remaining gaslight-free is being mindful about how, in general, you're living your life. Are you constantly preoccupied by the last fight you had with your boyfriend, your mother, or your boss? Or are you focusing on the life *you* want to lead: a life of integrity, fulfillment, and joy? Gaslighting takes up a tremendous amount of our mental, emotional, and spiritual energy. Committing to using that energy for the goals and dreams that really matter can help keep us gaslight-free.

New Possibilities to Celebrate
- You have the opportunity to keep your life gaslight-free and go on to a new future.
- You have a chance to rework or leave unsatisfying relationships and choose new relationships that feed your sense of self, vitality, and joy.

- You have a chance to become a stronger, more solid person who charts **your** own course and lives by **your** own values.
- Most important, you have the chance to discover what you truly want—in your work, your home life, your relationships, and yourself. Freed from the Gaslight Effect, you can make better choices, choices that are right for you.
- You can be your best self.

And once the storm is over, you won't remember how you made it through, how you managed to survive. You won't even be sure, whether the storm is really over. But one thing is certain. When you come out of the storm, you won't be the same person who walked in.

—Haruki Murakami

9

A Call for Joy

Congratulations! During your personal, hopefully illuminating, and at times difficult journey you explored what gaslighting is and the **telltale signs** that indicate you may be involved in a gaslighting relationship. To help focus your personal experience, I guided you through the **progressive stages of gaslighting** and the **three most common types of gaslighters**. During this exploration you were asked to delve deeply into your private thoughts and feelings, and I am humbled by your willingness to be vulnerable and all your hard work.

I hope the following overview helps highlight some of your key takeaways. My goal is to provide a simple review of a complex topic to help you recover the powerful and resilient person you are, remember what you discovered, and re-engage with yourself and others. My hope is that you are reinspired to find your joy and the freedom to express your most powerful potential and creative self.

It is a call for joy.

Developing a strong, clear sense of yourself and your self-worth is everything. Include yourself in the circle of people you have compassion for. In this chapter we are going to explore . . .

- Relationships that feed your sense of self, your vitality, and your joy.

- Becoming a stronger self, someone who charts your own course and lives by your own values.
- Discovering what you truly want.
- Making choices that are right for you.
- How to be your best self.

Birds make great sky-circles of their freedom.
How do they do it?
They fall, and falling, they're given wings.

—Rumi

Highlights: What Is Gaslighting?

Gaslighting is always the creation and interplay of two people.

1. The Gaslighter sows confusion and doubt.
2. The Gaslightee is manipulated into doubting their own perceptions to keep the relationship intact.

Remembering: Your Personal Highlight

What was your first feeling when you read this definition of Gaslighting? Did you embrace the idea as potentially important or push it away as inapplicable?

What does your response suggest to you?

_____

_____

_____

_____

A Call for Inspiration: Your Words of Wisdom—*What do you want to share? Write it down for ongoing inspiration. For example: "My mother told me that when you are arguing with someone, never say the one thing you know will **really hurt** them."*

_____

_____

_____

Highlights: The Three Stages of Gaslighting

In recalling how gaslighting works, remember there are three stages. At first, it may be relatively minor, and you may not even notice it. Eventually, though, gaslighting becomes a bigger part of your life, preoccupying your thoughts and overwhelming your feelings.

Stage 1: Disbelief—You may have a vague sense that something is wrong, but you can't quite put your finger on it.

You'd like to win your gaslighter's approval and have them affirm what a good, capable, and lovable person you are, but you can live with the idea of not being able to do this.

Stage 2: Defense—You are constantly defending yourself, ruminating over who is right and who is wrong. You can't stand the idea that you might have to walk away—even from an argument—without their approval.

You lose your ability to make judgments or to see the big picture, focusing instead on the details of your gaslighter's accusations.

Stage 3: Depression—You are more isolated, often depressed, and avoid talking about your relationship with others. With your gaslighter, you do your best to avoid anything that might trigger the gaslighting.

The gaslighter needs to be right and you need their approval, so you chose to blame yourself. You begin to feel nothing you can do will make a difference and can't imagine what will make you happy. You feel flat and numb.

Remembering: Your Personal Highlight

As you become more familiar with the three progressive stages of gaslighting, does one sound or feel more familiar to you?

Do any of the earlier stages also ring a bell? Can you remember when you may have moved from one stage to the next?

Rediscover Your Voice—Remember the strong self you can be—someone who charts your own course and lives by your own values. Ask yourself these questions.

- *What choices seem right for you at this point in time?*
- *What personal values direct your choices and the way you live your life?*
- *What values do you hold closest to your heart?*
- *What in your life inspired those values?*
- *Being true to yourself, what do you want to say? How will you say it? (You can*

write it, sing it, compose a poem, draw it, or simply speak it softly and clearly from your heart . . .)

A Call for Inspiration: Your Words of Wisdom—Scattered throughout this workbook are inspirational quotes from poets, philosophers, and thought leaders. **Now I'm asking you to tap into your own creativity and to be your own inspiration.** What are your words that will encourage you to live by and strengthen your core values, to be your best self?

*The most common way people give up
their power is by thinking they don't have any.*

—Alice Walker

Highlights: The Three Types of Gaslighters

1. **The Good-Guy Gaslighter—When you can't quite say what's wrong.** The Good-Guy gaslighter gets their own way while trying to convince you that you're getting what you want.

2. **The Glamour Gaslighter—When they create a special world for you.** They refuse to take responsibility for their hurtful or thoughtless behavior while sending the conflicting message that you must accept and enjoy their seemingly generous and romantic gestures.

3. **The Intimidator Gaslighter—When they bully, guilt-trip, and withhold.** This gaslighter urgently needs to be right, no matter the topic. When they feel challenged, they evoke the Emotional Apocalypse—a terrifying combination of yelling, insults, and reckless behavior that leaves the gaslightee scared and confused.

Remembering: Your Personal Highlight

When you contemplate **caring less** about what the other person thinks of you, does it feel doable? What other feelings come up when you think about caring less about your gaslighter's opinion?

Draw the **gap** between caring too much about what they think and caring more about what you feel.

What can you do to close that gap? Think of what you can do in the short term and the long term. Positive self-talk belongs in both categories!

_____

_____

_____

What are the **barriers** that stand in your way?

_____

_____

_____

What can you do to address those barriers?

_____

_____

_____

What could bring joy to this relationship? This may be a challenging question, especially if you are deep in the Gaslight Effect and it's been a long time since you have experienced joy. Give yourself a few minutes and be patient while looking for possible moments of joy.

_____

_____

_____

_____

_____

A Call for Inspiration: Your Words of Wisdom—In the space provided, be your own inspiration. What are your own words that will encourage you to live according to your core values and to be your best self?

_____

_____

_____

Highlights: The Gaslight Tango

A gaslighting relationship always involves the active participation of two people. You can end the gaslighting as soon as you stop trying to win the argument or convince your gaslighter to be reasonable or that you are right. Instead, you can simply opt out (and tolerate the pull to try to change their perceptions).

You have a deep source of power within you to free yourself from the Gaslight Effect. The first step is to become aware of your own role in gaslighting.

Why Do We Go Along with It?

Fear of the Emotional Apocalypse

The Emotional Apocalypse is an explosion that flattens everything in its vicinity and can poison the atmosphere for weeks afterward.

The Urge to Merge

No matter how strong, smart, or competent we are, we often feel an urgent need to win the approval of the gaslighter whom we've idealized and allowed ourselves to need.

When we feel anxious about disagreements or disapproval, we tend to respond in one of three ways.

1. We quickly align ourselves with our partner.
2. We might try to induce our gaslighter—through arguments and/or emotional manipulation—to come around to our own point of view.
3. We pivot to avoid the Emotional Apocalypse, after being worn down by our gaslighter's insistence and our protesting.

Remembering: Your Personal Highlight

If you have found yourself dancing a Gaslight Tango, do you **recognize** any of these dynamics?

Thinking about your personal dynamics, how would you **describe** some of your gaslight-prone responses?

_____

_____

_____

_____

Can you see how **your responses** may be contributing to the **Gaslight Tango**?

_____

_____

_____

_____

What is the **gap** between where you are now (comfortable with the familiar) and stopping the tango to create a healthier dynamic?

_____

_____

_____

What can you do to **close** that gap?

_____

_____

_____

What are the **barriers** that stand in your way?

_____

_____

What can you do to address those barriers?

_____

_____

_____

Remember, dancing the Gaslight Tango crushes joy. Keeping that in mind and looking toward the future, what could bring joy to this relationship?

Highlights: The Explanation Trap

This is **any effort to explain away behavior that disturbs us,** including gaslighting. We find seemingly rational explanations to prove to ourselves why these danger signals aren't really dangerous. The Explanation Trap can be very handy, but handy may not be healthy or even helpful.

Remember what goes on during gaslighting: Your gaslighter—even if they are capable of genuinely relating to you some of the time—becomes overwhelmed by their own need to restore their sense of self and sense of power by proving to you that they are right and insisting that you agree.

You may try to explain the behavior away, crafting a reassuring explanation that makes you entirely responsible for everything that goes wrong. This means that presumably you are entirely capable of fixing it.

Consider that you may be missing what your gaslighter really needs in the moment—and that this is the root of their gaslighting. You may mistakenly think you alone can "fix" what is wrong.

Let's take a moment to reflect . . .

What are the first explanations that spring to mind for your gaslighter's behavior?

_____

_____

What are the reasons for believing your explanation?

_____

_____

Could there be another possible explanation?

_____

_____

What are your Flight Attendants signaling or telling you?

_____

_____

Stopping the Dance Once It Has Begun

How Do You Stop It? These are useful suggestions at any stage of gaslighting but are especially effective during **Stage 1**.

- Don't ask yourself, "Who's right?" Ask yourself, "Do I like being treated this way?"
- Don't worry about being "good," just about being "good enough."
- Don't debate what you know to be true.
- Always tell yourself the truth about yourself.

Remembering: Your Personal Highlight

Which of these suggestions for stopping the tango feels the **most comfortable** to you?

_____

_____

Do they feel **doable**?

_____

_____

_____

What is the **gap** between where you are now and the doable actions?

_____

_____

_____

What can you do to **close** that gap?

_____

_____

_____

What are the **barriers** that stand in your way and what can you do to address them?

_____

_____

_____

_____

Recover Your Self-Worth and Build Resilience—Resilience is the capacity to adapt to, move through, and, ultimately, get beyond, emotionally stressful and challenging situations. It is the ability to flexibly build pathways toward well-being after a traumatic event or during extreme ongoing stress. It is not a character trait or magical quality that you are born with. There are many pathways of resilience, so the key is to find the path and strategies that will help you heal and move toward well-being.

Remember that healing is a unique journey. It is not about "bouncing back" but rather about "bouncing forward." There is no right or wrong way to do it, nor is there a correct timeline to follow. We are all unique individuals with different needs. It's important to know that optimum resilience is anchored in both a healthy body and a healthy mind. Let's begin with the ways we can support our body and mind to help strengthen resilience and have greater well-being.

The Resilient Body

- **Breathe**—Taking deep belly breaths is a good way to start. Slow, deep breaths relax the body and mind and activate our prefrontal cortex. This helps us feel calmer and problem-solve more effectively.

- **Sleep**—Getting enough sleep is linked to feeling and functioning better overall. Seven to nine hours a night can support clearer thinking, better decision-making, a more positive mood, and better emotion management.

- **Eat**—Food is fuel for our body and mind. It affects our mood, and mood can affect what we eat. Experts recommend eating whole foods and a blend of protein, fat, and carbs. Enjoy comfort foods in moderation.

- **Move**—Exercise gives us energy and strengthens our bodies, helps prevent disease, and strengthens the immune system. Find a way to move your body that works for you every day!

The Resilient Mind

- **Let Go**—Remain flexible in the face of adversity. Reassess, let go of what you need to, and then adjust to keep moving forward.

- **Find Strength**—Identify the strength in yourself and others that helped you through this challenging time.

- **Positive Self-Talk**—Talk positively to yourself. The way you tell yourself a story, and your part in what happened, is a reflection not only of your resilience but is also a pathway toward healing.

- **Love More**—During times of great stress, your heart may be opened to the healing power of love and nurturing. Reach out to others and spend time with people you love and who treat you with respect. Being socially connected is key to navigating stressful times.

- **Take Pause**—Take the time to reflect on and embrace your truth. Only a clear-sighted understanding of the situation and what you want can help you adapt and make new changes.

- **Make Meaning**—Reflect on what has happened in a truthful manner. Ask the questions you could have asked any day during this relationship, but didn't. How can you make your life more meaningful based on new wisdom?

Resilience through Feelings

- Give yourself permission to feel all your feelings.
- Skillful recognition and regulation of your feelings will help you through.
- Expressing your thoughts and feelings, and being open to other's feelings, strengthens bonds and promotes closeness.
- Use the power of positive emotions to nurture a positive view of yourself.
- Feed your hopeful feelings for the future.
- Allow gratitude to begin every day.
- Show your appreciation for those who are helping.
- Be kind to yourself when you backslide. Accept your mistakes and get back on track.

Resilience is common—it's how most people respond to challenging experiences.

—Dr. George Bonanno,
professor of clinical psychology at Teachers College,
Columbia University, and author of *The End of Trauma*

Remembering: Your Personal Highlight

Think about what would be different in your life if you took more time for self-care and nurturing your resilience.

What is one new thing you can commit to trying?

_____

_____

_____

A Call for Inspiration: Your Words of Wisdom—In the space provided, please be your own inspiration. What are your own words that will encourage you to live according to your core values, to be your best self?

_____

_____

_____

Highlights: Why Do We Stay?

Five Major Reasons People Stay in Gaslighting Relationships:

1. **Material Concerns**—Would you be able to maintain your current lifestyle? How important is that to you?

2. **Fear of Abandonment and Being Alone**—Do you believe you are still capable of finding a truly loving relationship? Do you want to?

3. **Fear of Humiliation**—What would your friends and family think if you left the relationship?

4. **The Power of Fantasy**—What is the fantasy of your relationship that might be hard to let go of?

Something to consider: Those who are prone to gaslighting are often compelled by three fantasies.

1. *Our partner (gaslighter) will be our sole source of nurturing.*
2. *We can change them through the sheer force of our tolerance, love, and example.*
3. *We are strong enough (or forgiving or nurturing enough) to transcend any unwanted behavior.*

Instead of the gaslighter's bad behavior making us like them less or feel less connected, it offers yet another chance to prove how strong we are. But we need to be wise enough, and humble enough, to gather our strength at perhaps our lowest point, to be our own parent and to take care of ourselves.

5. **Exhaustion and Depletion**—When you are exhausted or depleted, you don't think as clearly and don't make the best decisions. It's hard to focus—either on your own feelings (which are numbed anyway) or on what others are telling you about your relationship.

Courage is not simply one of the virtues
but the form of every virtue at the testing point.

—C. S. Lewis

Gaslighting Yourself Is Self-Sabotage

Gaslighting yourself prevents you from pursuing positive change. After all, if you don't believe your situation is that bad, you won't take action to change it.

Trash "Self-Talk"—Ways we use gaslighting to trash ourselves with self-talk.

- You minimize your own feelings.
- You constantly blame yourself.
- You doubt yourself.
- You are your own worst critic.
- You question yourself, including your memory.

This may sound familiar, since it is very similar to how you feel if you are being gaslighted by someone else. However, in this case *you* are the perpetrator. We convince ourselves that something is true when it is false. We embrace our doubts and are blind to our strengths and potential.

To challenge this habitual way of thinking, first notice when you have adopted a negative and self-critical mindset and then take action to embrace your positive and powerful self.

Voices of the Adults—Remember that our self-talk usually starts in childhood and often is a result of the way others talked to and about us as children.

- *As you think about the adults from your childhood, who comes to mind for you?*
- *What is your first feeling when you remember them?*
- *What does their voice sound like and what are they saying to you?*
- *Do you remember how you felt then? How are you feeling now as you remember?*
- *As you reflect on your personal negative "self-talk," what is your most familiar voice saying?*
- *Whose voice is it?*
- *What would you like to say to them in response? (Please write it down.)*

Embody Your Response: Give Voice to Your Words—Now, let's embody those words and give voice to your response. Let your body be your teacher. In difficult relationships, it's often hard to say "no," because "no" is more than just a word—it is a full sentence. Practicing giving voice to your thoughts can be helpful and freeing.

Now we are going to give voice to your response. *"No!," "No I'm not!," "No I'm not lazy!,"* or anything else that feels appropriate to you, like *"I'm a good person!"*

- Bring to mind a situation where you want to respond "no" or "no, I am not . . ." to someone. This can be a time where you recall that you wanted to and didn't—or a conversation you imagine having in the future.
- Notice how you are standing or sitting and how your body feels.
- Speak your chosen response naturally.
- Now repeat it a **little louder.** (Notice how it feels to speak your response with more authority.) Describe the feeling.
- Now repeat it again, **as loud as you would like.** How does that feel?
- Notice the position of your body now. Hold the position. Does the position feel familiar?
- Let your body complete its position like a dance (following your energy and body's lead).
- *Simply be the observer—do not judge yourself or what you are feeling. Now shake it out like a ragdoll while hopping up and down! And then stop, breathe deeply, and relax.*

A Call for Inspiration: Your Words of Wisdom—In the space provided, please be your own inspiration. What are your own words that will encourage you to live according to your core values and to be your best self?

_____

_____

_____

_____

Your River Story
Remembering Joy in Your Life

Let's revisit your chapter 1 River Story. We are going to reimagine the touchstones and defining moments that surfaced for you. In chapter 1, we were exploring whether your voice and reality were supported or crushed. Now we are going to remember moments in your life that brought you **joy.**

Defining Moments, Key Touchstones, and Feelings

Take a step back and look at your River Story.

1. Observe the defining moments over the past few years and up to the present that have shaped your life for better or worse. Include both moments when you were joyful and moments when your joy was not met or was crushed and became misery.

2. Close your eyes, get comfortable in your seat, relax, and take a few long deep belly breaths to release any extra energy and come to center.

3. When you feel complete, go back to the beginning, and, holding your key takeaways, gently answer the following questions.

Today's Date:

Beginning of your RELATIONSHIP:

Were there moments that were joyful for you?

_____

_____

Do you remember how joy felt in your body and mind?

_____

_____

When was the last time you experienced joy?

_____

_____

What are the details of the times you experienced joy—the people, the places, the activities?

_____

_____

What can you do now to bring more joy into your life?

_____

_____

A Call for Joy

What would you like to freewrite about now? How was it for you to write about joy—to think about bringing more joy into your life? There is wisdom in the teaching that **seeing children smile** can bring you joy, **giving** can bring you joy, **loving** can bring you joy, **inner peace** can bring you joy. What else can you imagine bringing you joy?

If, after the exploration of gaslighting and remembering joy, you realize you want to bring joy back to the relationship you are in, go for it! If joy was never a part of it, or you can't imagine joy in your future, listen to that information as you finish your review here.

Highlights: Turning Off the Gas

Let's review the techniques for setting limits, connecting to the values you hold dear, and strengthening your internal core of self-respect and resilience—the first steps to turning off the gas. You can't turn off the gas until you've fully prepared yourself to take action.

The only thing that will help your relationship change is your deep commitment to having a life you want—a life that is gaslight-free. Both you and your partner need to know that you will not stay in a relationship where you're not being treated with respect and where you're punished for having your own point of view.

Taking Action

1. Preparing Yourself to Act
2. Turning Off the Gas

Empowering Yourself to Act: A Six-Point Plan

1. Identify the gaslighting, set your priorities, and make a plan.
2. Give yourself permission to make a sacrifice.
3. Check in with your feelings every day.
4. Get in touch with your values.
5. Empower yourself, gather your resources, and surround yourself with love.
6. Take one step to improve your life. Then take another.

Keep a mindful eye as you move forward, asking what's working and what's not. And remember to give yourself compassion.

Remembering: Your Personal Highlight

Which of these six steps gives you the **most uplifting feeling**? Which do you most want to do?

List **your strengths** that will be particularly helpful to taking the steps successfully.

Turning Off the Gas—Here are five things you can do to help alter the dynamic between you and your gaslighter.

1. Sort out truth from distortion. Write down your last conversation and see where it pivots to gaslighting.

2. Decide whether the conversation is really a power struggle. If it is, opt out.

3. Identify **your** gaslight triggers, and **theirs**.

4. Focus on your feelings instead of who is right or wrong.

5. Remember that you can't control anyone's opinion, even if you're right! You can control your response.

Remembering: Your Personal Highlight

Which of these five actions feels the **most relevant** to your gaslighting dynamic?

Which of these five actions feels the most **doable**?

What **barriers** may get in your way?

What can you do to **address** those barriers?

A Call for Inspiration: Your Words of Wisdom—In the space provided, be your own inspiration. What are your own words that will encourage you to live according to your core values and to be your best self?

_____

_____

_____

Don't wait. The time will never be just right.

—Napoleon Hill

Highlights: Choosing Your Next Step

You may have already decided what you want to do. But if you haven't, we are going to review once again how to approach making this difficult decision.

Four Questions to Ask about Going or Staying

1. ____ Can I act differently with this person?

2. ____ Are they capable of acting differently with me?

3. ____ Am I willing to do the work it might take to change our dynamic?

4. ____ Realistically, if I give it my best effort, will I be happy with our relationship?

Remembering: Your Personal Highlight

When you contemplate acting differently (for example, letting go of your need to convince your gaslighter that you're right), does that feel doable?

If not, what are the barriers that might get in your way?

What can you do to address those barriers?

Trying to Change a Gaslighting Relationship from Within: Seven Things to Do

1. **Shift** to your integrity mindset.

What values are key for you to live by? _____

_____

_____

_____

2. **Be committed**—The only way your gaslighting dynamic will change is if you change it.

How will I alter my behavior? _____

_____

_____

3. **Be aware**—Check in with your own feelings and notice your responses, both emotional and behavioral.

What is it like to be me for a day? What does that tell me? _____

_____

_____

4. **Be honest**—Hold the long view.

Is there an overall pattern to how I feel most of the time? What is my primary feeling over the duration of a month? _____

_____

_____

5. **Be disciplined and use your emotion skills**—Identify and use your most helpful emotion regulation strategies.

What will I do to manage my emotional reactions so I can behave and respond differently to my gaslighter? _____

_____

_____

6. **Be responsible**—Take responsibility for your own part in the dynamic and decide what you want to do if you find yourself in a Gaslight Tango.

In the moment, what will I acknowledge to my gaslighter about what my actions may have triggered? _____

_____

7. **Be compassionate**—Extend compassion to yourself and your gaslighter. Your compassion may not alter your decision to leave or stay, but it will alter your tone.

What do I have compassion for in myself? _____

_____

_____

What do I have compassion for in my gaslighter? _____

_____

_____

Trying to Limit a Gaslighting Relationship: Seven Things to Do

If you want to limit a gaslighting relationship while remaining in it, these are the steps I encourage you to take:

1. **Be analytical**—Make a list of all the situations and/or topics that potentially trigger gaslighting in your relationship.

Potential triggers for you: _____

_____

_____

Potential triggers for your gaslighter: _____

_____

_____

2. **Be specific**—Using your trigger analysis, decide several specific ways and times you can set boundaries and/or get some distance.

What are the limits I have set? _____

_____

_____

What are the barriers to those limits? _____

_____

_____

How will I address the barriers specifically? _____

_____

_____

3.   **Be creative**—Before deciding that something can't be done, see if you can come up with a creative way to work around the problem rather than confront it head-on.

What are some creative ways I will set limits? _____

_____

_____

4.   **Be kind and firm**—Remind yourself that you have the right to set any limit you want and to maintain it as calmly and kindly as you can.

How can I stay calm to set us up for the most positive outcome even as I set boundaries? What emotion regulation strategies can I use? _____

_____

5.   **Be disciplined and use your skills**—Be consistent and steady with your message about the limits you want to set. Use emotion regulation strategies when needed. Think carefully about that message.

What specific message do I want to convey? _____

_____

_____

6.   **Be committed**—You will need to invest extra energy in making sure you get what you want, knowing that you may face a certain amount of opposition.

Imagine and describe the energy you are willing to invest in getting what you want. ____

_____

_____

7.   **Be compassionate**—Show compassion to your gaslighter and yourself. You are suffering and both of you will make mistakes. Try to view yourselves with compassion, even as you proceed with the tough decisions that you may need to make.

How will you show compassion to yourself and your gaslighter? _____

_____

Trying to Leave a Gaslighting Relationship: Four Things to Do

1. **Be in the present**—Stay in the present with your emotions. Projecting emotions into the future is often not accurate. The future is as mysterious and full of possibilities as it always was.

What are you feeling now that you have made your decision about what you want to do?

_____

_____

What gives you joy to think about in your future? _____

_____

_____

2. **Be receptive to help** and allow yourself to reach out. Ask for support from others you trust. Reaching out and accepting support makes us stronger and lets others know we trust them.

What are you going to do to bring comfort and serenity? _____

_____

Who will you reach out to for conversation and insights? _____

_____

_____

3. **Be patient**—You've taken a huge step toward making the changes you seek. But you can be sure they won't all happen immediately. Have patience, even when you feel otherwise. Keep breathing and allow yourself a bit more time to complete the process you've begun.

What do you need right now? _____

_____

_____

4. **Be compassionate**—Showing compassion can bring healing to both you and your gaslighter. Accept that you've done the best you can and offer yourself the compassion you deserve.

How will you stop your negative self-talk? _____

_____

_____

Commit to not saying hurtful or unforgiving things to your gaslighter. _____

_____

_____

Visualizing Your Relationship: Current, Past, Future

Once again . . . how would you answer this important question?

Realistically, if I give it my best effort, do I think I will be happy in our relationship? Will our life together bring me joy?

Be Your Best Self—What personal values will be your guide? *Please remember what is important to you in living a life worth living.*

Freedom Words

- In the space provided, freewrite a cluster of words that describe human **emotions, aspirations,** and **values**. Don't overthink this. Just let it flow without judgment. Use as many words as you would like.

_____   _____   _____   _____

_____   _____   _____   _____

_____   _____   _____   _____

_____   _____   _____   _____

- Take a step back and look at the word cluster. Let them all resonate with you personally.
- Circle the words you want to **live into**—words that inspire how you want to live going forward.
- Which of these feel the most natural for you to live by? Which words will feel the most difficult? Why?

No matter what you choose to do—change, limit, or leave your gaslighting relationship—reflecting on these questions will give you more insight. And acting on your insights will require your commitment to living a gaslight-free life. Please remember to be gentle with yourself and to move at your own pace. Sometimes responding to these questions brings up uncomfortable feelings.

The greater the difficulty,
the more the glory in surmounting it.

—Epicurus

Highlights: Bringing Closure

Hopefully you now understand your own role in the Gaslight Tango, and you've found new ways to step away from it. You've learned how to turn off the gas and you've decided whether to leave your gaslighting relationship, limit it significantly, or try changing it from within. Re-empowered, you can now focus on *keeping your life gaslight-free.*

What's Next? Let's take a quick look at your personal highlights and reimagine how you plan to accomplish your goal.

What Is Your Intention Going Forward?
- You are trying to change your relationship from within. _____
- You are trying to limit the intimacy of your relationship. _____
- You are committed to leaving the relationship altogether. _____

Do you still agree with your decision? _____ Yes _____ No

Does that decision give you joy? _____ Yes _____ No

If it doesn't, which decision will give you the most joy?

_____

_____

_____

_____

Forgiveness is just another name for freedom.

—Byron Katie

Remembering: Your Personal Highlight

Re-engaging with Yourself

- Has a part of yourself gone missing in this relationship? What part is that?
- Imagine the best possible way to re-engage with that part of yourself.
- Commit to taking one step and then another in order to make this happen.

Remembering Your Joy—What do you truly want? What joy do you want to breathe in? What unpleasant energy do you want to release from your body and breathe out? Let me share a wonderful breathing meditation with you.

- Sit quietly and take a few deep belly breaths to relax and center yourself. Close your eyes if you're comfortable; if not, gaze softly downward.
- Imagine your joy as a glowing light surrounding you. Watch it become brighter. Does it have a feeling or a color? Begin to breathe in that joy and allow it to fill your entire body, up to the top of your head and down through the tips of your fingers and toes. Hold the breath and embrace the experience.
- As you begin to breathe out, switch your focus by relaxing and gathering all the unpleasant energy you would like to release from your body. Let it out in one long, firm breath through your open mouth. Notice if your energy has a color or a feeling.
- Enjoy the new space that releasing the unpleasant energy has opened in your body. Fill this space with joy as you take your next breath.
- Repeat the in-breath and out-breath as often as it feels good to you. Then gently bring the meditation to a close by filling your body with joy. Set the intention to carry this joy within you as you go forward into your day.

The Unexpected Gift—Imagine that you are sitting with a trusted friend who has come to dinner to celebrate and support you on your journey to creating a gaslight-free life. Having shared much of your experience with this friend, it has been a huge comfort to openly share many of your thoughts and feelings throughout the difficult process.

- They have surprised you by bringing an unexpected gift! It's a small package that you begin to unwrap carefully. It appears to be a cotton T-shirt with some words printed on the front. As you unfold the T-shirt, your heart leaps and dances with joy. You exclaim, *"Oh my god, you really see me! You really get me!! Thank you!"*

• What does your T-shirt say? _____

To Bring Us Full Circle . . . At the beginning of the book, I asked you to respond to some provocative comments. Now, after working through this book, I invite you to provide your "after" responses to those same comments. Hopefully, your responses will make you smile and reflect on your hard work and commitment to living a gaslight-free life.

Your After Responses . . .

1. "You're overreacting, and everybody knows it!"
Your response now:

_____

_____

_____

_____

2. "You're being irrational . . . again. I'm just telling you this for your own good."
Your response now:

_____

_____

_____

3. "If you were a considerate partner, you would have made sure you got there before the store closed." Your response now:

_____

_____

4. "I never said that to you. You must be starting to lose your memory."
Your response now:

_____

_____

5. "Can't you see how those guys are looking at you? You know you're flirting—just admit it." Your response now:

_____

_____

_____

Bringing Closure . . .

The key to remaining gaslight-free is not to let your self-worth depend on someone else's approval. Developing a **strong, clear sense of self** and **self-worth** is crucial to **strengthening your resilience** and will help you stay out of gaslighting relationships.

The Opportunity for Joy Is Yours

- Create a gaslight-free life and go on to a new future.
- Rework or leave unsatisfying relationships and choose new relationships that empower your sense of self, your vitality, and your joy.
- Become the stronger, more creative and confident person you can be, who charts **your** own course and lives by **your** own values.
- Discover what you truly want—in your work, your home life, your relationships, and yourself. Freed from the Gaslight Effect, you can make better choices, choices that are right for you.
- Be your best self. Live a life worth living.

Dance, when you're broken open.
Dance, if you've torn the bandage off. . . .
Dance when you're perfectly free.
—Rumi

Gaslighting in the Workplace

Case Study—Marlene, a smart, hardworking assistant director at a midsize pharmaceutical company, was feeling confused and insecure. She had a great personality and was well liked by her colleagues. Her supervisor consistently praised her to her face, lauded her in group meetings, and put her name forward for interviews. And yet, she had been passed up for promotion over and over again. She finally set up a meeting, gathered her courage, and told her supervisor . . .

"I'm confused. I should be up for a promotion. I haven't gotten one in three years, and I was on track before the pandemic. I don't know why it's not happening, and I'd like to discuss this. In fact, today at lunch I heard from Rayna that she is going to move into the open executive director position."

Marlene took a deep breath. Before she could continue, her supervisor interrupted to tell her for the umpteenth time how valuable she is to the organization and urged her not to worry. Then he went on and on about how fabulous Rayna had been over the past year and how deserving she was for a promotion. Marlene's supervisor ended the meeting and suggested they meet again in a few months. In the meantime, he suggested again that Marlene "not worry at all." Marlene left the meeting smiling and felt momentarily relieved . . . until she realized that there was no conversation about *her* being promoted—it had all been deflected. Her supervisor had simply gone on and on about Rayna. Maybe she was wrong to worry; maybe she was too obsessed with titles; maybe she didn't deserve a promotion; maybe she had taken the wrong approach with her supervisor.

Some Warning Signs of Gaslighting in the Workplace

Gaslighting may not involve all of these experiences or feelings, but if you recognize yourself in any of the following statements, give it extra attention. *(Check the signs that feel familiar.)*

☐   You are constantly second-guessing yourself.

☐   You ask yourself, "Am I too sensitive?" a dozen times a day or "Am I being paranoid?"

☐   You often feel confused and even crazy in interactions with your boss or colleagues.

☐   You may feel socially isolated from others and don't know why.

☐   You are ruminating about conversations with your gaslighter.

☐   You are always apologizing.

☐   You can't understand why you aren't happier when you have such a good job.

☐   You feel burned out and exhausted.

☐   You can't remember when you last felt motivated.

☐   You can't understand why you don't feel respected when your boss or colleague says they do respect you.

☐   You frequently make excuses for your boss's or colleague's behavior.

☐   You know something is wrong, but you don't know what and assume it must be you.

☐   You start lying to your boss or colleague to avoid put-downs and reality twists.

☐   You have trouble making simple decisions.

☐   You don't recognize yourself.

☐   You wonder if you are good enough at your job.

☐   You wonder if you are a good enough employee or colleague.

☐   You are working far from your full potential.

☐   You can't seem to find your motivation.

☐   You feel stuck in the same place, unable to move ahead, and don't know why.

What Does Gaslighting Look Like in the Workplace?

What the Gaslighter Does: Manipulates, lies, deflects, denies, isolates, and gossips to gain control of others' perceptions of their target. They never admit they are doing any of it.

If you feel like you have lost your grounding or that you are being undermined in your workplace, someone could be gaslighting you. It could be a power-hungry colleague, a defensive manager, a jealous coworker, a prejudiced team member, or an unhappy customer or client. *Their actions may include one or more of the following:*

1. **Isolate or Exclude You:** Gaslighters may leave you out of meetings or drop you from group emails to make sure you get less and less information, direct contact, or validation from anyone other than the gaslighter.

For instance: You are suddenly dropped from a regular meeting and notice that you are invited to fewer professional social gatherings.

Making It Personal—In Your Own Words...

Does this feel familiar? Can you think of an example where you may have been excluded from meetings, gatherings, or information loops?

_____

_____

_____

_____

---

2. **Ignore You:** Gaslighters may ignore you in meetings or forget to give you credit.

For instance: You co-led a successful project, but when the project was mentioned in the meeting, your name was not.

Making It Personal—In Your Own Words . . .

Does this feel familiar? Are you beginning to feel you should be questioning your contributions in the workplace?

_____

_____

_____

3.   **Talk Negatively About or Discredit You:** Gaslighters may put down your work and suggestions in public and sometimes tell you directly that you don't know what you're talking about.

    For instance: Your boss directly insults you or your work in a meeting.

Making It Personal—In Your Own Words . . .

Does this feel familiar? Can you think of any specific examples where your boss insulted or embarrassed you in front of others or caused you to question your value as a team player?

_____

_____

_____

4.   **Lying or Denying:** Gaslighters will outright lie to make their target less sure of themself, pretending (even in outrage) to have assigned one task, when they really assigned another.

    For instance: Your boss creates a false narrative by telling a story and omitting important facts to make you look bad.

Making It Personal—In Your Own Words...

Can you think of any examples where you suspect your boss misled others about your considerable contributions?

_____

_____

_____

5. **Intimidation:** The gaslighter is a workplace bully, using credentials and personal power to get their way. Gaslighters may even use a threatening physical presence (e.g., towering over, blocking the doorway) to deliver a gaslighting message.

For instance: You refrain from speaking up or disagreeing with your boss because you fear their temper.

Making It Personal—In Your Own Words...

Can you think of any specific examples where you were frightened by your boss's behavior or implied threats? Please take a moment to describe them, even if you know it may be painful to revisit.

_____

_____

_____

6. **Creating Fuzzy Boundaries:** Gaslighters may encourage your "urge to merge" and invite you to join them in their reality, knowing you want to be in sync "together."

For instance: Your boss may ignore personal boundaries and invite closeness. As the more powerful person in the relationship, the gaslighter may start making more decisions *for* you.

Making It Personal—In Your Own Words . . .

Can you think of any examples where your supervisor cajoled you into permitting them to make choices for you while pretending it was a joint decision?

_____

_____

_____

Which Statements Feel Familiar?

____ Your boss tells you about yourself all the time; most of the feedback is negative.

____ Your boss tells you that your complaints are no big deal or that you are too sensitive.

____ Your boss praises you to your face, but you have the feeling that they are undermining you behind your back.

____ You feel there's nothing you can do to please your boss.

____ You used to feel competent at work and now you don't.

____ You're always checking out perceptions with your coworkers. After you leave work, you're constantly replaying conversations you had with your boss, but you can't figure out who's right or remember what they said—but you know you felt attacked.

Progressive Stages of Gaslighting in the Workplace: The gaslighting may remain the same, but over time your experience of being targeted and having to put up with it may cause you to descend through the following stages and behaviors.

The Three Stages of Gaslighting

Stage 1: Disbelief—You're surprised when your supervisor gives you a bad performance review since you are a tireless and conscientious worker. But you listen attentively to their "constructive criticism" and take action to change the achievable. Eventually, as your supervisor continues to criticize your performance with more certainty, you begin to question if they might be right. Stage 1 gaslighting is insidious. It can be profoundly destabilizing and undermining. You may have a vague sense that something is wrong—but you can't quite put your finger on it. *Do any of these feel familiar?*

____ You'd like your boss to recognize what a good, capable, and professional person you are, but you can live with the idea of not being able to do this.

____ You begin with your own sense of self and point of view, and when they say something that seems incorrect, you might present your own opinion.

____ When your boss behaves in a hurtful or bewildering manner, you wonder, "What's wrong with them?"

____ You consider your own point of view normal and theirs as mistaken, distorted, or outrageous. But you begin to have a nagging feeling that they may be right about you.

____ You make judgments about what's going on. You're not sure you can work for someone who gets so upset about such petty things.

Stage 2: Defense—You are constantly defending yourself, ruminating over recent interactions with your supervisor, and wondering how you can convince them that you are a team player and excellent employee. You can't stand the idea that you might have to leave this great job, especially before you have gained their approval. However, if you don't continually agree with them, they might use the Emotional Apocalypse: yelling, finding more pointed criticisms, or giving you less attention, feedback, and fewer assignments. Now, when your boss overreacts, you no longer wonder, "What's wrong with them?" *Do any of these feel familiar?*

____ You really want to win their approval—it's become the only way you feel confident. You may argue out loud or in your head, but you think of their opinion first.

____ When they behave in an insulting or bewildering manner, you wonder, "What's wrong with me? Why can't I see what I've done wrong?"

____ You consider their point of view to be normal and wish desperately to get a hearing for your own perspective. You can't bear the idea that their criticisms may be true, so you'll prove the one thing that really matters to you: you are a good, capable, and valuable team player because your boss agrees that you are.

____ You lose your ability to make judgments or to see the big picture, focusing instead on the details of their condescension and accusations.

Stage 3: Depression—After you've been gaslighted over a long period of time, you lose touch with the strong person you were when you began the job. You feel more isolated and alone at work, and you even stop talking about your boss with others. You do your best to avoid anything that might trigger your boss's gaslighting behavior. In this stage, you often take on their perception and assessment of you and keep track of evidence that they are correct in their negative view of you. *Do any of these feel familiar? If so, you may be dancing the Gaslight Tango.*

____ You depend on the gaslighter for your professional reputation and desperately want to win their approval.

____ Even though you have a good job, you feel lonely, confused, and frustrated, but can't say why.

____ You have lost hope for finding a way to get your boss to agree with you.

____ You look for ways to prove your gaslighter right at the expense of your self-esteem.

____ You are still making feeble attempts to show your gaslighter that they have misunderstood you and should think about you differently.

____ You feel flat, numb, and joyless at a job that used to bring you inspiration.

Why Do You Put Up with It?

1. **Fear of Losing Your Job and Identity**—For many, our job is a big part of our livelihood and sense of personal power. It's the difference between maintaining independence and

being dependent on others. Losing one's independence can be an unbearable situation for many productive and self-motivated individuals.

2. **Fear of Abandonment**—In the workplace, relationships with colleagues and hard-won accomplishments are an important part of maintaining a strong sense of self and personal purpose. To lose this important connection to others and ourselves is tantamount to forfeiting one of our most important and strongest adult attachments.

3. **Fear of Retribution**—Professionals work hard to behave respectfully when navigating the workplace hierarchy. But survival of the fittest can be a slippery slope when departmental flowcharts are constantly changing. A small misstep could trigger a deluge of reputational retaliation and unfair punishments.

4. **Fear of Anger and the Emotional Apocalypse**—The open expression of anger can be intimidating to those who are not familiar with it or those who have suffered from its violent results. An explosion of rage can flatten everything in its vicinity and poison the atmosphere for weeks afterward. It can be such a painful experience that the gaslightee will do anything to avoid it. Giving in completely—in thought and emotion as well as action—may seem like the only safe course.

5. **Desperation to "Right" the Gaslighter's "Wrong" View of You**—You feel unable to let go of the idea that you need to walk away, even if you can't fix the gaslighter's perception of you. You understand you can't control anyone else's thoughts, but you feel you can't let go until you convince the gaslighter that they are wrong and you are right.

Making a Plan: How Should You Respond to Gaslighting?

Current Needs—First, let's look at your current need to stay in this work relationship so we can begin to make a plan. Consider the **key drivers** in your personal and work life right now.

Economic Need . . . *For example: "To support myself and my dependents."*

What is *your* economic need? _____

_____

_____

_____

_____

Psychological Need . . . *For example: "To achieve my professional and personal goals. To bolster my positive self-image, personal happiness, and joy."*

What is *your* psychological need? _____

_____

_____

_____

Reputational Need . . . *For example: "To preserve my professional reputation in the workplace and create a positive and true story for my résumé."*

What is *your* reputational need? _____

_____

_____

_____

Preparing to Turn Off the Gas

1. Identify the problem/name the behavior.
2. Give yourself permission to make a sacrifice.
3. Get in touch with your feelings.
4. Take one step to improve your life. Then take another.

Taking Action: Give Yourself Agency and Self-Respect

1. **Identify the problem and when it happens**—Identifying gaslighting gives us the possibility to see it clearly and to reframe what happened.

Name the Behavior. Awareness of your boss's manipulative behavior helps you see the situation clearly and take action to protect yourself, reframe your responses, and improve the potential for positive outcomes. Knowing your boss's gaslighting patterns can help you figure out what you can and cannot tolerate.

What my **gaslighter** does to gaslight me:

_____

_____

_____

What **I do** as a target:

My behavior: _____

My feelings: _____

My thoughts: _____

2. **Give yourself permission to make a sacrifice**—Consider that you may need to leave your job, even if you don't have to. Leaving your gaslighting relationship may cost you something. Thus, being willing to leave (*even if you don't actually end up leaving*) often means facing the prospect of tremendous loss. The point is, you don't know. Your gaslighting relationship is unlikely to get better if you do nothing. The only hope for change is to act differently. Yes, you may be risking something of great value if you do that. But you have to decide if making the change is worth it to you.

3. **Check in regularly with your feelings**—Focus on feelings instead of being "right" or "wrong." Just being able to name and then speak your feelings helps you connect with them—and with the energy to stand up for yourself. So does expressing your feelings in a different way.

Draw Your World

Now take this opportunity to create your Workplace Sociogram. Complete instructions for this wonderful visual tool can be found on pages 124–125. This time, we will focus on mapping your personal working relationships and discover more information about your interpersonal space, energetic ties, and feelings for each person. Here's an example:

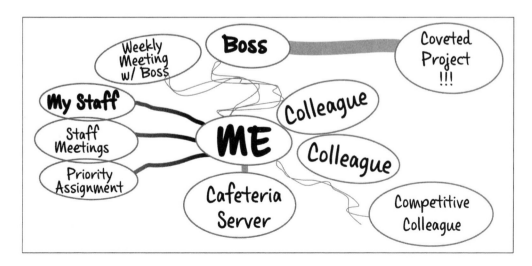

Awakening Your Feelings

Jot down your answers in any form you like—sentences, brief notes, or anything else that works for you. You can also draw or diagram your answers.

Recall the last event that had an emotional impact on you. It could be as major as getting a new job or as minor as a disagreement with a bank teller. Describe the incident.

_____

_____

_____

What did you feel?

_____

_____

_____

What did you think?

_____

_____

_____

What did you do?

_____

_____

_____

4. **Take one step to improve your life. Then take another**—It's amazing how powerful it is to take an action—any action, even a small one—that will make your life better. Even if your action seems to have nothing to do with your job situation, taking it will help you mobilize to turn off the gas.

Taking Action: Personal Empowerment

The sense of empowerment from taking action can help move you to challenge your gaslighter. It may feel difficult to turn off the gas because, after weeks, months, or years of being gaslighted, you're often not the same strong self you were when you entered your gaslighting relationship. Restoring that empowered self to take action is a powerful tool in your mobilization to turn off the gas.

What would you like to do first? What gives you an undeniably pleasant feeling when you think about doing it?

_____

_____

What are the **barriers** that stand in your way of doing what you just wrote about?

_____

_____

What can you do to overcome those barriers? Are you willing to do that?

_____

_____

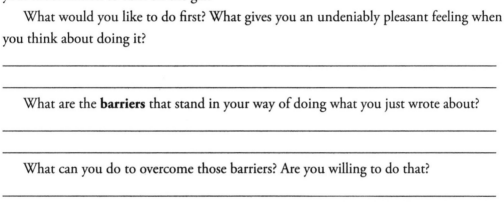

Five Ways to Turn Off the Gas

1. Follow professional protocols and protect yourself.
2. Sort out truth from distortion.
3. Decide whether the conversation is really a power struggle. If it is, opt out.
4. Identify gaslighting triggers and patterns.
5. Identify how far your boss will go.

Protecting Yourself in the Workplace

1. **Follow Professional Protocols**
    - **Document Communications**—Write things down and keep accurate records of communications, especially with your gaslighter.
    - **Be Smart**—Schedule all meetings (no informal chats), create an agenda, and take notes.
    - **Get Support**—Try to include a third person in meetings to witness communications and get another perspective.

2. **Sort Out Truth from Distortion**—Often our gaslighters tell us their version of events, and we get completely thrown. There's just enough truth in their version to make us think that the whole package is true. Sorting out the truth from the distortion can be a helpful step in turning off the gas. Write down conversations and interactions.

List your gaslighter's criticisms and accusations. To prepare and clarify your thoughts, write them down in the space provided . . .

My gaslighter's accusations . . .

_____

_____

_____

_____

_____

_____

_____

Step back and look at the accusations. Being your own best friend, check the ones that you admit have some grain of truth to them.

Reflecting on the ones you checked (and being as honest as you can), get in touch with your honest motivations, needs, and performance. **Can you separate your truth from the false accusations of your gaslighter?** Write those realizations down.

*My gaslighter's distortion (accusations and assumptions that are not true)
versus my truth (my real motivations and needs).*

_____

_____

_____

_____

_____

_____

3. **Is It a Conversation or a Power Struggle?** Gaslighting is so insidious that you don't always realize what the conversation is really about. The difference between a power struggle and a genuine conversation is that in a genuine conversation, both people are really listening and addressing each other's concerns, even if they get emotional at times.

If you are not arguing about the actual incident, you can be sure you are enmeshed in a power struggle. And if it's a power struggle, you can choose to opt out.

You Know It's a Power Struggle If...

It includes a lot of insults.

You keep covering the same ground without reaching a resolution.

You can't stand not being right and you need your colleague to see your point of view.

One or both of you bring in topics that are way off target.

No matter what you say, your boss or colleague has the same response.

You feel you are being bullied but without clear and productive goals.

Some things you can do to opt out

1. Take a deep breath and say nothing. Let your boss or colleague own the silence.

2. Say, "Respectfully, I disagree with you. If it's okay, I'd like to give it some more thought and circle back."

It's important to learn how to move beyond our strong and habitual impulse to beg for our gaslighter's approval—which may make them even more anxious or angry. We need to identify and practice ways to opt out of the power struggle.

Making It Personal—In Your Own Words...

Can you think of some opt-out statements that feel personal and doable for you? Write them down here.

_____

_____

_____

4.   **Identify the Triggers and Patterns**—You are in a Gaslight Tango with your boss or colleague, but you aren't sure what their trigger is. Knowing your gaslighter's pattern can be helpful.

Please take a minute to reflect on any comments or behavior on your part that seem to trigger your gaslighter's feelings of defensiveness and negative response. Have you made an honest mistake? Perhaps you are doing an exceptionally good job?

My Behavior Trigger: _____

Their Response:_____

My Behavior Trigger: _____

Their Response:_____

My Behavior Trigger: _____

Their Response:_____

5. **Identify How Far Your Boss Will Go and Identify the Consequences**—Does the gaslighting inevitably result in punishment—altered work assignments, docked pay, dismissal—or is it only a psychological game? Again, when you see the situation clearly, you can figure out your own limits and plan of action.

What kind of limits does your gaslighter have? Make a list of the gaslighting consequences you have observed.

They will:_____

They won't:_____

They will:_____

They won't:_____

They will:_____

They won't:_____

Set Boundaries—**What can you do?** Figure out how much contact you really need to have. Some bosses are central parts of our working lives; others function more as offstage figures. No one likes to be gaslighted by their supervisor, but the dynamic may be easier to live with if your job does not require you to interact with them daily.

Choose Boundaries Wisely: Create a list of work commitments that require you to engage with your boss or colleague and helpful ways to protect yourself, and keep that time gaslight-free.

Work Commitments: *Scheduled meetings, email exchanges, assignments, one-on-one team meetings, lunch meetings, and so on.*

Professional Habits: *Make an agenda, take notes, clarify goals, include a third person in meetings when possible, write down communications, and so on.*

Workplace Activities to Avoid: *Informal meetings alone, weekend meetings with fuzzy agendas, after-work drinks, and so on.*

A New Narrative for Building Resilience and Healing

- What is the story you will tell about this relationship or time in your life?
- What can you learn by looking at it from a new perspective?
- How can you make meaning out of this time?

Reappraisal—One of the most popular research-based strategies for "emotion management" *is positive reappraisal.* It's simply telling yourself a new story about a situation to help you see the situation in a more positive light.

Not only can reappraisal make us feel better and more positive, but it's also a socially helpful strategy that reaps rewards in the response we get from others.

Reappraisal is particularly necessary and powerful in the workplace.

Positive Reappraisal—Let's practice changing negative thoughts to create a more positive perspective and emotional impact.

Current Negative Thought: *"I can't win. I can't take this job another day. I'm totally unappreciated, so f— them all!"*

New Positive Perspective: *"This job is good for another two years. After that, I'm moving on to greener pastures anyway."*

Current Negative Thought: *"I hate it here and I'm exhausted. I give up—I'm such a loser."*

New Positive Perspective: *"I think I can still learn more from this work situation, so I'm going to grit my teeth and find a way to make it work. As long as I'm getting something positive out of it, I can take that to a better job."*

My Current Negative Thought:

_____

My New Positive Perspective:

_____

Positive Self-Talk—Most of us spend more time knocking ourselves down than lifting ourselves up, especially in gaslighting relationships. Positive self-talk is a way to coach yourself with love. What is the negative distortion of yourself that your gaslighter has instilled in you? Access a positive way to talk to yourself about the very same thing. For example, your gaslighter tells you, "You have no voice. I've never heard you make a constructive sentence." Your negative self-talk: "He's right. I'm such a loser." New positive self-talk: "I'm a good listener and I choose my suggestions wisely."

My Current Negative Self-Talk:

_____

My New Positive Self-Talk:

_____

Additional Notes: How can you turn more of your personal negative thoughts into positive and productive statements?

From: _____

To: _____

From: _____

To: _____

From: _____

To: _____

Quick Review: Your Steps to Deal with Gaslighting

As you are in the process of making a decision about what action you would like to take, let's take a quick look at everything we have discussed to help bring it into focus.

If you feel you are losing your grip and efficacy in the workplace:

Allow your feelings. If you feel uncomfortable, investigate further.

Describe your feelings as specifically as you can. _____

_____

_____

_____

Check in with your Flight Attendants. Check in with others you trust, who are good sources on respectful communication.

What are your Flight Attendants saying?

_____

_____

_____

What would your trusted friend say?

_____

_____

_____

Write down a conversation at work that left you feeling badly or confused.

Name it: You are not crazy. (Naming your reality in a gaslighting situation gives you the possibility to see it clearly and to reframe what happened.)

How can you reframe the conversation to have a more positive impact on you?

New Positive Perspective . . .

_____

_____

Are you gaslight-free or gaslight-prone?

Are you gaslight-free? _____ Yes _____ No

At Work—You are relatively confident about yourself and your work. What your supervisor thinks about you doesn't really penetrate deep into your sense of who you are. With that self-esteem you may be able to shrug off your boss's odd interpretation and avoid gaslighting.

Are you gaslight-prone? _____ Yes _____ No

At Work—If your sense of self depends on your gaslighter's approval, you might start to wonder if maybe they have a point. As soon as you begin giving space to their theories, knowing they are not true, you've opened yourself to further gaslighting.

Decide whether or not you are willing to have a conversation with your colleague or boss about your gaslighting dynamic.

If you decide to go forward, think of some ways you can frame the conversation positively.

Making It Personal—In Your Own Words . . .

Some things you can say . . .

_____

_____

_____

Decide what you will do if the gaslighter flatly denies their behavior or gets more defensive and accusatory.

What would you like to do? Consider if you are willing to leave your position or limit your relationship? Think of some things you can say to clarify your thoughts and next steps that would have the most positive outcome for you.

Making It Personal—In Your Own Words . . .

Some things you can say . . .

_____

_____

_____

Give yourself permission to limit your contact with this person or leave if the situation is too toxic or unmanageable.

Making It Personal—In Your Own Words . . .

Some things you can do . . .

_____

_____

_____

Now, What's Your Plan?—Let's review the highlights of your decision and the specifics on how you plan to accomplish your goal.

What's Your Decided Objective?

____ You are trying to productively change the relationship with your gaslighter.

____ You are trying to limit the relationship productively.

____ You are committed to leaving your job altogether.

Do you still agree with your decision? _____ Yes _____ No

Does that decision lift you up? _____ Yes _____ No

If it doesn't, what can you do to empower yourself?

_____

_____

_____

_____

_____

_____

_____

_____

_____

Keeping Things in Perspective

So now, how do you distinguish between a couple of bad days and a pattern of ongoing psychological manipulation?

1. On balance . . .
   - Do you feel heard, appreciated, and effective in the workplace? **Y / N**
   - Do you feel you're getting what you want? **Y / N**
2. Look to your Flight Attendants . . .
   - When you think about your work, do you feel joy, pleasure, and satisfaction? **Y / N**
   - Or do you feel anxiety, trepidation, and uncertainty? **Y / N**

Review—Finally, let's look at the big picture.

Making It Personal—In Your Own Words . . .

"Where am I now?"

_____

_____

_____

"Where would I like to be?"

_____

_____

_____

"What are the steps that I am going to take to get to where I would like to be?"

_____

_____

_____

"What are the barriers keeping me from moving forward?"

_____

_____

_____

"What are the steps I am going to take to address those barriers?"

_____

_____

_____

"What will my daily life at work feel like when I get there?"

_____

_____

Bringing Closure

The key to remaining gaslight-free is to ensure that your self-worth does not depend on someone else's approval—even your boss's. Developing a strong, clear sense of your self-worth, your performance, and your value to the company is crucial to staying resilient and avoiding toxic gaslighting relationships.

The Opportunity for Joy Is Yours

- Create a resilient gaslight-free life at work and a future full of clarity and well-being.
- Rework, limit, or leave unsatisfying relationships and choose new work environments that empower your sense of self, vitality, and joy.
- Become a stronger, more creative, and confident person who charts **your** own course, lives by **your** own values, and works to your full potential.
- Discover what you truly want—in your work, your home life, your relationships, and yourself. Freed from the Gaslight Effect, you can make wiser choices, choices that are right for you.
- Be your best self and always treat yourself with compassion.

You are your best thing.

—Toni Morrison

The Family Case: Gaslighting at Home

Gaslighting in families is a special and confusing case. Most of us will put up with almost anything to stay connected. We have a shared history and are deeply invested in our family group. We may hold on to a belief that our family will always (or should always) be there for us, to support us emotionally and love us unconditionally. And, almost always, they are the ones who have taught us who we are and how to be in the world. Even when this isn't true, severing these connections can feel impossible—it may seem like you are cutting off part of yourself.

As you move forward, looking at the interpersonal dynamics in your family, you will explore what you are comfortable doing, what you **want** to do, some options for what you **can** do, and **how** you can do it.

Most important, remember to be gentle with yourself. Although families can be a source of love, they can also cause deep emotional pain.

Case Study—Meredith always envied her cousins, who were well-dressed and went to the finest schools. Whenever they got together on holidays, she would compare herself to them—but each time, she came up short. She knew that there were many things she didn't know about the world they grew up in: the world of money, connections, and accessibility. It wasn't that her own family wasn't great, but Meredith could never decide for herself whether that was the right pathway to success in life. She just knew that the way her family lived was different than her cousin Brittany's family. And, when she was honest about her feelings, she hated being so envious.

She thought her own mom was great: she was actually pretty cool with her casual style and informal manner. She was a voracious reader of nonfiction and had accumulated an amazing amount of knowledge over the years. Not only did Meredith think of her mom as wise, all her friends loved her too. But she still wished her mom had the means and access her aunt had. It would have made all their lives so much easier.

As Meredith grew up, she thought a lot about which way was the right way to live. She forgot to think about what she wanted and instead got lost trying to figure out the "should." And it didn't help when conversations with her aunt would leave Meredith second-guessing herself.

Here's one example from her uncle's fiftieth birthday party.

> **AUNT SUSAN:** "Meredith, how nice to see you!"
>
> **MEREDITH:** "Thanks, Aunt Susan. It's been a long time! I'm so glad every-one's here. I love your necklace."
>
> **AUNT SUSAN:** "You know, I really admire you, Meredith—you and your mom. You really don't care how you dress! Look at you, wearing workout clothes. That's real freedom."
>
> **MEREDITH:** "Thaaanks ... Aunt Susan." [Meredith thought this over, trying to figure out if this was a good thing or a bad thing.]
>
> **AUNT SUSAN:** "Meredith, I tell it like it is—you can count on me for telling you the truth. You really don't care. If you did, you would dress differently. You're one of the lucky ones."

But wait, Meredith thought. I do care. I care too much. But she is saying I don't care, because of the way I'm dressed. I know I used to think she was nuts, but maybe she's right. But why do I feel so shitty about it?

We all grow up in a family. And families can look very different. Single parents, two moms, raised by grandma, not blood relatives but still my family—families come in all shapes and sizes. Within this constellation of people are all types of relationships: close and critical, close and nurturing, unpredictable, distant but warm, distant and cold.

Some of these relationships support who we are and how we see the world, and some don't.

What Does Gaslighting Look Like and Feel Like in Families?

1. **It looks like power.** "I am your mother, and I am telling you . . ."
2. **It looks like certainty.** "Oh *excuuuse* me . . . I think I have a few more years of experience here."
3. **It looks like repetition.** "How many times do I have to say you are a slob before you believe me? Just look at that pigsty of a room."
4. **It feels like humiliation.** "Why fight so hard to get the car tonight? You know no one at the school cares if you show up."
5. **It feels destabilizing.** "I never said that. You're making it up—and no one likes a liar."
6. **It feels minimizing.** "What's your problem . . . So what if I did that? It's no big deal—you're way too sensitive."
7. **It feels like a direct attack.** "You don't know how to think, do you? You can't seem to make a decision."

Making It Personal—In Your Own Words . . .

What does gaslighting feel like in your family?

_____

_____

_____

_____

The Three Stages of Gaslighting in Families

In families, the gaslighting stages look different than when you first meet someone as an adult and they say something that gives you pause. In fact, there are usually no stages—in families, the gaslighting might just be the air you breathe. By the time you are old enough to think and respond, you may already be dancing the Gaslight Tango with a parent, sibling, or relative. Or you may have been taught by your parents to second-guess yourself and to check with them to know what reality is.

Parents and caregivers frame and control the world a child lives in. They tell their child how to interpret the environment around them; they define what reality is and what it is not. A child will look to their parents to help make meaning out of conversations and behavior. They inform a child's general knowing of how the world works and how people operate in it.

And the very people—the moms, dads, and other adults who raise you—who teach you about yourself and who love and care about you, are the same adults who choose how to manage their anxiety and gain control of an interpersonal moment, sometimes by (unknowingly) gaslighting you and undermining your experience and reality.

It could look something like this

- "You don't hate your baby brother—you love him!"
- "You don't even like cold weather. You are not going to enjoy ice skating."
- "You're a quiet person; you can't possibly like Judy—she's too outgoing for you."
- "You don't really want to stay home tonight—you just forgot how much fun you have with Aunt Millie."

Or it can be more devastating

- "That school is not for you. That's a school for smart girls, like your sister. You don't belong there."
- "You may have fooled them, but we all know you're worthless."

Making It Personal—In Your Own Words . . .

What are some statements you have heard that might have caused you to wonder if you really felt one way or the other, or if you were even capable of knowing yourself?

_____

_____

_____

_____

Let's Look at the People You Grew Up With—Gaslighters in your family might be loving and caring, hovering over you with warmth and interest. Sometimes they are aggressive and intimidating; other times they are steady and reliable. They can be your loving mom, your fun dad, your caring grandma, your upbeat sister, your curious auntie—but they always insist that their reality is *the* way the world works, *the* way people should behave, and *the* way you are.

Your Family Sociogram

Let's create a **Family Sociogram**. A sociogram visually charts relationships within a group at a given point in time. In this case, we're mapping your personal group of family relationships.

By placing relationships in visual proximity to you, based on their emotional closeness and importance in your life, the sociogram will provide more information about your interpersonal space, energetic ties, and feelings for each person.

Ready, Set, Draw: Get your drawing tools and let's get ready to create your family sociogram. I'll remind you of the steps.

> ✔ You can use color, size, and distance and embellish your circles and lines any way you want to reflect *how this relationship really makes you feel* and the *frequency or intensity of interactions*.

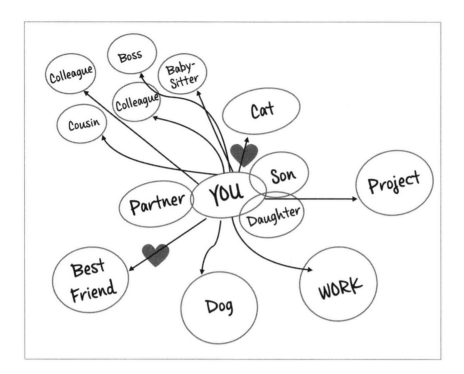

✔ First, **draw yourself in the middle of the page.** Represent yourself with a circle or another shape, a line drawing, or simply words.

✔ Then begin drawing circles (with names), representing relationships in your family as they spontaneously come to mind. *(Don't overthink this; it's a bit like automatic writing.)*

✔ Draw their circles in proximity to you based on how you feel about them right now.

✔ Now draw an expressive and directional line between you and them.

✔ Continue to build until you feel satisfied, allowing the drawing to take on a life of its own.

✔ Now take a step back and look at your drawing. Observe the location of where you placed your relationships in proximity to you. Notice how you feel about the placements.

✔ Then imagine that you are floating way up high to observe your family sociogram from your hot-air balloon. Allow memories to surface of specific interactions and feelings that prompted you to draw a particular circle-relationship exactly where you put it.

As you draw, consider the following: *Thinking about the home you grew up in, who were the people who supported your belief in yourself and your reality? Who were the people who challenged your reality, your beliefs, and your perceptions?*

Your Space:

Unpack Your Sociogram—Step back and look at it. Are the people you placed around you where you would like them to be? On reflection, are there any you would like to be closer or farther away?

How will you get there? _____

_____

_____

Signs that you may be in a gaslighting relationship within your family:

____ Your parents' or relatives' perception of you doesn't match your perception of yourself, and they're happy to tell you about it.

____ Your siblings are constantly accusing you of behavior or attitudes that you don't believe you have.

____ Your siblings have an image of you and of themselves that you just don't see, and they insist that you share it.

____ Your siblings insist on treating you as though you were stuck in your childhood role. If you're the youngest, they treat you as if you are still acting like a baby; if you're the oldest, they behave as though you are still bossing them around.

____ You're frequently defending yourself.

____ You feel like you're never doing enough.

____ You feel like a bad kid for asking for something.

____ You find yourself feeling guilty more often than not.

Gaslighting Example: "Mother on a Bus"

I was riding on the bus some time ago and witnessed a gaslighting interaction that left me feeling helpless and sad. It left me wondering if there will be a time when the child involved will hear another voice—a voice that validates or supports him in holding onto his reality.

> **MOM:** "Sit still. What's wrong with you?"
>
> **YOUNG BOY:** [*Looking in his backpack*] "I am just..."
>
> **MOM:** "Just stop it. I told you not to make any noise; just sit in your seat!"

YOUNG BOY: "But Mom, I'm hungry . . . I'm just looking for some candy. I'm so hungry." [*He keeps looking.*]

MOM: "There's something wrong with you. You don't listen. Good boys listen!"

YOUNG BOY: "But Mom, I just want a piece of candy. I just want something to eat."

MOM: "Good boys listen. Are you listening? No. Not you. Good boys listen."

What's the message here? He is not a good boy, because good boys listen. He isn't listening. His mom said so. That is her reality. But what is his? Because his mom—whom he deeply trusts—said this was true, therefore it must be so.

Voices of Your Childhood

Childhood is replete with direct and indirect messages from parents, grandparents, siblings, and the extended family. And what your family tells you goes on shapes the messages that you tell yourself—about your own self. In this way, negative talk can become negative self-talk, and without a deliberate decision to turn that negative self-talk into positive self-talk, you can diminish yourself every day into adulthood—sometimes before you get out of bed in the morning.

"You're the pretty girl—your sister is the smart girl."

    Self-Talk—"I am not smart."

"You are so lazy—you'll never amount to anything."

    Self-Talk—"I am lazy—I need to push harder."

"Look at yourself. No more ice cream for you, young lady."

    Self-Talk—"I'm too fat."

"You're worthless—everyone knows it."

    Self-Talk—"I am worthless."

"You're so selfish—nobody is going to love you."

    Self-Talk—"I am not loveable."

"You're too loud; it's not ladylike."

    Self-Talk—"I am too loud/too much."

First Thoughts—Making It Personal. *I want you to write the first thoughts that come to mind about who you really are and how you feel. Don't overthink this. It's like speed writing. Just let the thoughts flow without editing them in your mind.*

Self-Talk—I am _____

Self-Talk—I am _____

Self-Talk—I am _____

Self-Talk—I am _____

Self-Talk—I am _____

Self-Talk—I am _____

We've been talking to ourselves since we were little, integrating not only everything our parents told us about ourselves (good and bad), but also the comments that other people around us have made. These beliefs become part of our self-image that we carry into adulthood.

Sadly, some of us are gaslighted into believing something about ourselves that may have started as a deliberate manipulation by our parents. They might have inadvertently gaslighted us in an effort to diminish something that was upsetting or over the course of trying to discipline and control our behavior.

For example: *In an effort to diminish your negative feelings, Mom says, "You're not really hurt by that; you're just feeling crabby and hungry."*

Alternately, in an effort to build up your self-confidence, your parents may keep telling you how brilliant you are.

For example: *"You are brilliant! Don't worry—people will see how smart you are!"*

If you believe them, you are inadvertently being set up to enter a hardworking and competitive world with a false sense of self. Alternatively, if you know you aren't brilliant, you may suffer from feelings of inadequacy and experience the imposter syndrome.

Examples of self-talk I hear from my patients who believe their gaslighters:

"It's true—I am provocative."

"I'm perfect just the way I am, and if you don't see it, you must be blind."

"I don't know how to listen—even though I thought I was listening."

"Why should I have to exert myself when my natural superiority speaks for itself?"

"I am lazy."

"I am stupid."

"My good looks will get me what I want in life."

"I'm not smart enough."

"I'm the smart one."

"I'm the 'creative' one, which means I can't cut it with the Ivy Leagues."

"No one will love me for who I am."

"My older brothers are much smarter and stronger than I will ever be."

"I am 'too much' for anyone to put up with."

"I am a nightmare."

"I am a lunatic."

"I am bad; I get out of control."

"I'm self-centered and such a bore."

"I am not fun enough."

"I am not sexy/pretty/attractive."

"No one really cares about me—except him."

Check In with Your Reality—*What are you still hearing from your own childhood?*

What did you learn from your parents about who you are in the world? _____

_____

_____

What are the words you remember from your childhood? _____

_____

_____

Whose "voice" is it? _____

_____

_____

Do you still replay the words as self-talk? **Y / N**

How does it impact your life now as an adult? How do these words show up in your

behavior? _____

_____

_____

How can you turn those self-critical statements into positive thoughts?

From: *"I'm hopeless when it comes to numbers and creating a budget."*

To: *"I'm a work in progress. I'm going to keep trying and find a way to make it fun."*

From: _____

To: _____

From: _____

To: _____

From: _____

To: _____

From: _____

To: _____

Naming gaslighting gives us the possibility to see the manipulation more clearly and act on our own behalf.

> **GRANDMOTHER:** "*Everyone* is coming up here to help me next weekend. I was counting on you, Stacy. I am very disappointed in you and won't forget it."
>
> **STACY:** "You know, I really want to come, and you know I always do when I can. It would be so much easier for me to help out in the family if I was

included in the scheduling. I don't think I am being selfish—I'm just busy and wasn't consulted."

GRANDMOTHER: "You don't think of yourself as selfish? I need you next weekend, not when you feel like getting involved. I have told you this so many times. You always have had your own selfish priorities, haven't you?"

Stacy accepted the accusation—after all, her own self-interest stood in the way of her coming through for Grandma. She began to think of herself that way, and it took many months and the help of a counselor for her to let go of her need for Grandma to change her opinion, and to stand firm in seeing herself as not being selfish even though Grandma said she was.

By naming the gaslighting, she was able to see clearly and no longer take it to heart. Going forward in a perfect world, she would have liked to be honest and to talk to her grandmother about the gaslighting dynamic, but she knew that would not be possible. Instead, in her own mind, she was able to reframe it with compassion when her grandmother was nasty or critical. For example, she might say, "She can't help herself; she doesn't know another way to manage disappointment. I can move beyond it for the sake of family harmony."

It's helpful to remember to take a deeper look at the motivation that triggers gaslighting behavior.

- **When you disagree with them**—remember there is certainty on their end.

- **When you disappoint them**—it is easier for them to blame and gaslight you than to deal with real feelings of disappointment.

- **When your relative wants to avoid or deny responsibility**—maybe they have overpromised and don't want to deal with that.

- **When they feel accused or in the wrong**—it is easier to blame you (your sanity, your character, etc.) than to take responsibility.

- **When they feel anxious and out of control**—they need to re-establish control.

Positive Reappraisal

Let's take another look at *positive reappraisal*. Simply telling yourself a new story about a situation to help you see the situation in a more positive light can change the emotional impact of a potentially negative situation.

Reappraisal can not only make us feel better and more positive, it's also a socially helpful strategy that reaps rewards in the response we get from others.

Let's take a look at Jodi's story as an example.

Jodi was waiting for her sister Donna in line at the movies. Donna was almost forty-five minutes late, Jodi had already bought the tickets, and the movie was about to start. Jodi was pissed. "This always happens. She is so inconsiderate. She thinks the world revolves around her." Jodi was emotionally charged. She took a deep breath to calm down and reverse the physiological effects of her feelings. Short breaths, flushed cheeks, sweaty palms. Jodi decided to tell herself a new story.

"I feel pissed and impatient, but I do know that later I will be glad to see her and she is my sister—I don't think she will ever be any different. Even when she's late, I always enjoy our time together."

Jodi used a helpful strategy to shift herself into a more pleasant emotional state. When Donna did show up, Jodi said nothing, and they both enjoyed the movie and pizza afterward.

But if we look at Jodi's situation a bit more closely, we see how the positive reappraisal can become a slippery slope to enabling and even encouraging unwanted behavior.

It was the umpteenth time Jodi was waiting for her sister. She couldn't even remember how many times she'd been waiting, but she did remember the money she spent on tickets and drink minimums for get-togethers that Donna barely made. She was so sick of the same situation. That day it was the movies, but it had already happened in comedy clubs, coffee shops, and even while waiting for a train to leave for a vacation they had planned together. By this point, she couldn't tell herself a more positive story. Even more outrageous was that Donna gaslighted her when she arrived there and said that Jodi was just so uptight!

But Jodi commits to using the reappraisal strategy just one more time. She's quieted her anger at Donna. And it did feel better in the moment. But she is aware that she no longer has the same upbeat, positive feelings about making plans with Donna. She reflects on the reality that they are family forever and she knows her sister was indulged and really does get everyone to revolve their lives around her.

For Jodi, limiting the amount of time she plans to spend with her sister seems to work for now.

Your Family River Story
Power of the Past: Visualization

I invite you to take a look at some key moments in your Family River Story. Please go back in your mind's eye to your early childhood and reflect on key moments as you travel the river of your life up to the present day. Following the instructions, look at moments when your inner reality was either encouraged or dismissed.

Your moment may be as simple as your mother telling a seven-year-old you that you weren't hungry, even when you were certain that you were.

Allow yourself to reflect on your childhood and growing up in your family—from as early as you can remember up to the present.

Close Up: Part 1 of Your Journey

- Write the date of your birth in the bottom-left corner of a blank page and today's date in the upper-right corner.
- Next, draw the river of your life between the date of your birth and today's date. It can be a straight line, have many twists and turns, tributaries or no tributaries—it's your decision.
- Now, close your eyes (if comfortable) or simply look down and imagine that you are on the bank of the river and getting into a hovercraft that will float two feet above the water. You will travel in your hovercraft following the river of your life from your birth up to the present date.
- As you float along, notice the touchstones beneath the water and allow them to represent those defining moments in your family life, when your perceptions and feelings were either encouraged or squashed. Note those defining moments emblazoned in your memory.

Take a few minutes to notice those defining moments. What do you feel? What comes to mind? Write or draw those moments in your river.

Big Picture: Part 2 of Your Journey

- When you feel complete, go back to the beginning and imagine that you are in a hot-air balloon retracing your journey from this higher perspective.
- As you move along between the defining moments of your life, allow yourself to remember more detail about those moments when your perceptions and feelings were either encouraged or squashed.
- Identify one or two of these moments from this new perspective that stand out for you right now. Spend a few minutes writing about these moments. What did you feel? What was the immediate impact? The long-term impact?

Defining Moments and Your Feelings

In the space provided please write or draw those defining moments and feelings that are emblazoned in your memory.

Today's Date:

Your DOB:

Notes: Now, as you reflect further, identify the top three defining moments that stand out for you right now and describe the impact they've had on your life.

What were the top three defining moments? Describe the interactions.

1. _____

_____

_____

2. _____

_____

_____

3. _____

_____

_____

What were your feelings and thoughts during those interactions?

1. _____

_____

_____

2. _____

_____

_____

3. _____

_____

_____

What was the message about yourself that you took away from that moment?

1. _____

_____

_____

2. _____

_____

_____

3. _____

_____

How did it impact you? Go back to your river. This time, floating high above the water in a hot-air balloon, notice the impact that that gaslighting moment may still be having on your life today.

1. _____

_____

_____

2. _____

_____

_____

3. _____

_____

_____

Steps to Deal with Gaslighting Moments in the Present

If you feel crazy or undermined in the relationship: *(Choose a specific family relationship you would like to work on in the following reflections.)*

Allow your feelings—if you feel uncomfortable, investigate further.

Describe your feelings as specifically as you can. _____

_____

_____

Check In with Flight Attendants—Check in with others you trust who are good sources on respectful communication.

What are your Flight Attendants saying?

_____

_____

_____

What would your trusted friend say?

_____

_____

Write down a conversation verbatim that left you feeling badly or confused.

Name it—You are not crazy. Naming your reality in a gaslighting situation gives us the possibility to see it clearly and to positively reappraise what happened.

Notice the triggers that lead to gaslighting with this person.

Examples of triggers: *Curfews, setting limits, money, visiting relatives, feelings and behavior about personal responsibility at home, and so on; list the occasions, topics, comments, or behavior that trigger the gaslighting dynamic.*

Think about if you are willing to have a conversation about the dynamic with your gaslighter.

What would you like to do? If you are willing to talk about it, think of some things you can say to describe your feelings and which would open the conversation positively. *For example, you might say to your sister, "Debra, you know how much I love you! You always have my back. But I'm a bit confused about what you said at dinner about this weekend. Without your ride home, I won't be able to go . . ."*

Making It Personal—In Your Own Words...

Some things you can say...

_____

_____

_____

Decide what you will do if the gaslighter flatly denies their behavior or it gets worse. *For example, your sister says, "You're making that up—I never said I'd pick you up. That was just wishful thinking on your part!"*

Making It Personal—In Your Own Words...

Some things you can say...

_____

_____

_____

Give yourself permission to step away for a time if it feels too toxic. *What are some things you can say to pave the way for you to stop the interaction or conversation and leave the room?*

Making It Personal—In Your Own Words . . .

Some things you can say . . .

_____

_____

_____

Give yourself permission to limit the relationship. *Make a list of helpful ways to limit the time spent with anyone in the family who tries to manipulate you. Make sure your plan is realistic.*

Making It Personal—In Your Own Words . . .

Some things you can do . . .

_____

_____

_____

Helpful Tools in Continuing a Difficult Relationship

Positive Reappraisal—How can you change the story you tell about the interaction to create a more positive perspective and emotional impact?

Negative thought:

_____

Positive perspective:

_____

Positive Self-Talk—What is the negative belief about yourself that they have instilled in you? Setting that aside, access your inner truth and express the positive and joyful potential that you know is the real you.

Negative thought:

_____

Positive perspective:

_____

Choose Activities Wisely—Make a list of activities you want to do and those to avoid as you set your personal limits with this family member.

Wanted Activities: *(List)*

Activities to Avoid: *(List)*

Be Your Best Self—As you begin to express your joy and embrace your best self, let's reflect for a moment. Let's focus one last time on where you are and where you would like to be. Bringing your family gaslighter to mind, please spend a minute reflecting on where you are in limiting or changing the dynamic and where you would like to be.

Summation Exercise

"Where am I now?"

_____

_____

_____

"Where would I like the relationship to be?"

_____

_____

_____

"What are the steps that I am going to take to get to where I would like to be?"

_____

_____

_____

"What will I feel like in the relationship when I get there?"

_____

_____

_____

"What are the barriers keeping me from limiting or shifting the relationship?"

_____

_____

_____

"What are the steps I am going to take to address those barriers?"

_____

_____

_____

Bringing Closure . . .

The key to remaining gaslight-free in any relationship is to not let your self-worth depend on someone else's approval. Nor should you believe their destabilizing and covert messaging. Developing a strong, clear sense of yourself and your self-worth is crucial to staying out of gaslighting relationships no matter where they are.

In a family, gaslighting can be even more confusing. These are the people who are supposed to love and protect you, and who also have the most impact on your developing beliefs and sense of self as a child. The gaslighting may be so pervasive that it has become your reality and the very air you breathe. Or it may simply be a dynamic between you and one other family member. Whether it's intentional manipulation "for your own good" or unintentional yet damaging messaging, it still chips away at your self-esteem and can leave you feeling confused and crazy. It may be difficult to leave the relationship even if it never changes, so it is even more important that you are able to recognize, change, or find a way to step away when the gaslighting happens.

The Opportunity for Joy Is Yours

- Create a gaslight-free or gaslight-limited life at home and experience greater well-being and a more secure sense of self within your family.
- Recognize, rework, or distance yourself from disempowering relationships. Choose to spend more time with family members that empower your sense of self, your vitality, and your joy.
- Step into the stronger, more creative, and confident person you can be—the you who charts **your** own course and lives by **your** own values.
- Discover what you truly want: in your home life, your familial relationships, and yourself. Freed from the Gaslight Effect, you can make better choices that are right for you.
- Be your best self and treat yourself and others with compassion.

The Quick Guide to Gaslighting

What Is Gaslighting? (page 1)

Gaslighting is an insidious and sometimes covert form of emotional abuse, repeated over time, where the abuser leads the target to question their judgments, reality, and, in extreme cases, their own sanity. It's a type of psychological manipulation in which a gaslighter—the more powerful person in a relationship—tries to convince you that you're misremembering, misunderstanding, or misinterpreting your own behavior or motivations, thus creating doubt in your mind that leaves you vulnerable and confused.

The Gaslight Effect results from a relationship between two people:

- A gaslighter, who needs to be right to preserve their own sense of self and to keep a sense of power in the world.
- A gaslightee, who is manipulated into allowing the gaslighter to define their sense of reality because they idealize the gaslighter and seek their approval. The gaslightee feels themselves slipping into confusion and self-doubt—but why? What has made them suddenly question themself? How has a person who supposedly cares for them left them feeling so awful?

The Three Stages of Gaslighting (page 6)

Gaslighting tends to work in stages. At first, it may be relatively minor—indeed, you may not even notice it. Eventually, though, gaslighting becomes a bigger part of your life, preoccupying your thoughts and overwhelming your feelings. Finally, you're mired in full-scale depression, unable even to remember the person you once were. You've lost touch with your own point of view and your sense of self. Of course, you may not proceed through all three stages. But for many who are susceptible, gaslighting goes from bad to worse.

Stage 1: Disbelief

You can't believe your partner is saying such silly things or trying to tell you there's something wrong with you or your actions. Eventually, as your partner continues to insist on their reality and undermine yours, you begin to question if they might possibly be right.

Stage 2: Defense

You are constantly defending yourself and ruminating over what you and your partner said to each other. Who is right? Who is wrong? You can't stand the idea that you might have to walk away—even from an argument—without their approval.

Stage 3: Depression

When you've been gaslighted for a long period of time, you're no longer the same person as when you entered the relationship. You are more isolated, you are often depressed, and you avoid talking about your relationship with others. With your gaslighter, you do your best to avoid anything that might trigger abuse. In this stage, you often take on the gaslighter's distorted and critical judgment of you.

The Three Types of Gaslighters (page 7)

1. **The Good-Guy Gaslighter—When You Can't Quite Say What's Wrong.** The Good-Guy gaslighter gets their own way while trying to convince you that you're getting what you want.

2. **The Glamour Gaslighter—When They Create a Special World for You.** They refuse to take responsibility for their hurtful or thoughtless behavior while sending the conflicting message that you must accept and enjoy their seemingly generous and romantic gestures.

3. **The Intimidator Gaslighter—When They Bully, Guilt-Trip, and Withhold.** This gaslighter urgently needs to be right, no matter the topic. When they feel challenged, they evoke the Emotional Apocalypse—a terrifying combination of yelling, insults, and reckless behavior that leaves the gaslightee scared and confused.

The Gaslight Tango (page 25)

A gaslighting relationship always involves the active participation of two people. You can end the gaslighting as soon as you stop trying to win the argument, convince your gaslighter to be reasonable, or prove that you are right. Instead, you can simply opt out and resist the pull to try to change your gaslighter's perceptions.

Let's take a closer look at the intricate steps of the **Gaslight Tango**.

Step 1. The dance usually begins when a gaslighter insists that something is true, despite your deep knowing that it is false. For example: *"You know you are so forgetful; you know that you are!"*

Step 2. Gaslighting can occur only when a gaslightee tries—consciously or not—to accommodate the gaslighter or convince the gaslighter to see things their way, because they seek approval. For example: *"I am not forgetful! I never miss an appointment! How can you say that? I have never even been late."*

Step 3. Rather than stick with their own perceptions, when a gaslightee is worn down, they try to win the gaslighter's approval by finding a way that the two of them can agree and be joined in their reality. They pivot. Most often, they pivot by giving in and accepting the other's reality at the expense of their own.

Why Do We Go Along with It?

1. Fear of the Emotional Apocalypse
2. The Urge to Merge

The Explanation Trap (page 60)

This is **any effort to explain away behavior that disturbs you,** including gaslighting. You find seemingly rational explanations to prove to yourself why these danger signals aren't really dangerous.

You're trying to pick and choose, deciding which part of the gaslighter's behavior to respond to and which part to ignore. Try to slow down your responses and be aware of your own behavior, feelings, and motivation. Ask yourself if you are caught in the **Explanation Trap**.

Here are four ways you might imprison yourself in the Explanation Trap.

1. "It's not him, it's me."
2. "He feels so bad."
3. "No matter how she behaves, I should rise above it."
4. "Unconditional love."

Stopping the Tango Once the Dance Has Begun

These are useful suggestions at any stage of gaslighting, but they are especially effective in **Stage 1**.

- Don't ask yourself, "Who's right?" Ask yourself, "Do I like being treated this way?"
- Don't worry about being "good," just about being "good enough."
- Don't debate what you know to be true.
- Always tell yourself the truth about yourself. Don't be afraid to empower yourself.

Why Do We Stay? (page 115)

There are six major reasons people stay in gaslighting relationships:

1. Material concerns
2. Fear of abandonment and being alone
3. Fear of humiliation
4. Fear of feeling shame
5. The power of fantasy
6. Exhaustion and depletion

Those who are prone to gaslighting are often compelled by three fantasies.

1. *Our partner (gaslighter) will be our sole source of nurturing.*
2. *We can change them through the sheer force of our tolerance, love, and example.*
3. *We are strong enough (or forgiving or nurturing enough) to transcend any unwanted behavior.*

Turning Off the Gas (page 128)

Here are five shifts that may help you alter the dynamic between you and your gaslighter:

1. Sort out truth from distortion.
2. Decide whether the conversation is really a power struggle. If it is, opt out.
3. Identify your gaslight triggers, and theirs.
4. Focus on feelings instead of who is right or wrong.
5. Remember that you can't control anyone's opinion—even if you're right!

Choosing Your Next Step—Decide Your Objective (page 169)

- **Change**—Are you trying to change your relationship from within?
- **Limit**—Are you trying to limit the intimacy of your relationship?
- **Leave**—Are you committed to leaving the relationship altogether?

APPENDIX B

Understanding the Behavior

Theoretical explanations from the perspective of **Relational Self Psychology** for "Taking It Deeper" were compiled in consultation with my esteemed colleague Chris Scott, LCSW-R, CGP, Clinical Director Village Counseling Center NYC, creator of the EmpathyWorks Learning Center (https://empathyworks.org/learningcenter), and teacher and therapist. Other theoreticians and practitioners whose work I have referenced include G. Atwood, J. Bowlby, B. Brandchaft, J. Fosshage, V. Gallese, M. S. Gazzaniga, D. O. Hebbs, H. Kohut, F. Lachmann, Les Lenoff, M. L. Livingston, D. Orange, R. Stolorow, and D. Winnicott.

Immediately following each "Taking It Deeper" box is a personal deeper-dive exercise called "Finding Yourself."

Exercises and Visualizations

Taking Care of Mind and Body

Getting Therapy and Other Kinds of Help

If you're feeling ready to consider a change—or at least to learn more about your options—you may decide that you would like some help. You may not know what you want, but you do know you are unhappy, uncomfortable, and need some space to sort things out. As a therapist myself, I suggest the following:

- Counseling or psychotherapy is one mode of supporting your self-discovery and growth. Therapy can be frustrating and painful at times—getting better doesn't always mean feeling better right away—but it can also be wonderfully nurturing and supportive. There is nothing like having a space and time set aside for someone to deeply listen to you; nothing like the relief of knowing that someone else understands your concerns and is committed to helping you reach your goals.
- Consider enlisting another type of helper or supporter. Life coaches, while usually not trained as therapists, can be good at helping you define your goals and supporting you while you take specific steps to reach them.
- Religious leaders and pastoral counselors can offer support and spiritual in-

sight (and some of them are also trained as therapists). You might join a support group at a local community center or at your religious institution.

- If you or someone close to you struggles with substance abuse or some other form of addiction, or if that is another challenge with your gaslighter, a twelve-step program might be right for you.

- No matter what kind of support you choose, I urge you to reach out to your friends and loved ones, at least to all those people whom you trust to have your best interests at heart and a clear view of your situation. (It can be hard, sometimes, to find people who meet both of those qualifications!) But sometimes, even the best of friends are not enough. Sometimes you need someone who stands a little bit outside your life to help you figure out the next stage of your journey. A therapist or another type of helper can be that "outsider" who helps you find the road back in.

An Antistress and Antidepression Diet

People struggling with gaslighting relationships also often suffer from stress and/or depression. As you figure out what's going on and what to do about it, it's important to take care of yourself. Consult a nutritionist or try the following antistress and antidepression diet, which may help you think more clearly and feel more empowered.

- Eat three meals and two snacks a day. Low blood-sugar levels can make you feel confused and hopeless, so keep your spirits up by eating at least every three hours. Make sure to include high-quality protein with each meal or snack, such as lean meat, fish, eggs, low-fat dairy products, nuts, or tofu.

- Eat plenty of whole grains, legumes, low-fat dairy products, fresh fruits, and vegetables. Grains, legumes, and dairy products help your brain manufacture serotonin and other vital hormones that fight depression and boost feelings of self-esteem and empowerment. Fresh fruits and vegetables provide key vitamins and minerals that your brain needs to think clearly.

- Make sure you're getting enough omega-3 fats, found in fish and flax. Studies have shown that omega-3s play a vital role in combating depression. The hormones they help produce support your self-esteem, feelings of hopefulness, and a sense of empowerment.

For more support on diet, I suggest checking out *The Chemistry of Joy* by Henry Emmons, MD, with Rachel Kranz; and *Potatoes, Not Prozac* by Kathleen des-Maisons.

Sleep for Empowerment and Mood Enhancement

Sleep is important and never more so than when you're in a stressful situation. You need all your resources to combat gaslighting, so make sure you're getting at least eight hours of sleep each night. If you're having trouble falling or staying asleep, try to develop a calming bedtime routine; avoid caffeine, other stimulants, and alcohol, even early in the day; eat a healthy carbohydrate snack (milk, fruit, nuts, cereal, whole-grain bread, or brown rice) about an hour before bedtime, and consider a natural sleep aid, such as valerian or melatonin.

Most Americans are relatively sleep-deprived and get at least an hour less sleep than they need each night. Just improving your sleep patterns may go a long way toward giving you the strength you need to think clearly and take new actions. However, if you're sleeping more than ten or eleven hours a day, you may want to restrict your sleep to eight or nine hours. In some cases, excess sleep feeds depression and supports a sense of sluggishness and lassitude.

Exercise for Empowerment and Mood Enhancement

The positive benefits of exercise are enormous. Exercise helps you release stress, build brain-healthy hormones, improve sleep, and generally increase your sense of self-empowerment and self-esteem. See if you can give yourself at least fifteen minutes a day of mild aerobic exercise—a brisk walk will do. If you can, work your way up to thirty minutes a day, five days a week. If this feels like an impossible goal, start small. Even a five-minute daily walk will make you feel better than you do now. And if you're already getting regular exercise, good for you! That is one positive step you are taking to support your brain chemistry, your emotional balance, and your sense of self.

Hormonal Cycles and Antidepressants

Our bodies and brain chemistry have a great impact on how we feel, which is why I've suggested paying attention to diet, exercise, sleep, and other physical factors in your mood.

You may also want to consider how hormonal issues are affecting your mental and emotional condition. Some women have intense responses during the premenstrual portion of their cycles or during ovulation, times when you may feel either more despairing about changing your situation or more desperate about wishing to change. You may find yourself changing your mind about whether you want to make changes—and whether you have the energy to make changes—depending on where you are in your cycle. Many women also experience intense feelings in response to the hormonal fluctuations of perimenopause and menopause.

If you feel that a hormonal imbalance may be making it more difficult for you to see your situation clearly, you might seek the help of a physician and/or an alternative practitioner. A medical doctor can prescribe hormone replacement therapy or other supplementation. A naturopath, nutritionist, or herbal healer (including many acupuncturists and specialists in Chinese and Ayurvedic medicine) can suggest natural products that might help balance your hormones. (The herb pau d'arco, available as a capsule, tablet, or tea, is one of the most potent. I have friends who swear by it.)

If you feel that your brain is foggy and your emotions are out of whack, you may want to see a physician or psychiatrist about prescribing antidepressants. Antidepressants should always be taken in conjunction with a brain-healthy diet and exercise plan, such as the one I've just outlined. They should always be taken in conjunction with a therapist's care, and they should never be seen as a long-term solution. But they can bring you some short-term breathing room in which you can see life from a more empowered, upbeat place.

On Mindfulness

Struggling with the effects of gaslighting can be exhausting, depleting, and confusing. Cultivating a mindfulness practice and making it part of your daily routine (or even your bedtime routine) can improve your overall well-being. A mindfulness practice requires that you focus your attention on the present moment—accepting and noticing thoughts and feelings in the here and now, without judgment. Mindfulness can help lower your physiological activation, increase your mental clarity, and encourage you to adopt a wider perspective on your life, in contrast with gaslighting, which is notorious for keeping us stuck in fuzzy rumination. Mindful meditation techniques have roots in Buddhism and are very popular today, not only among single or group practitioners but also in schools, workplaces, spas, and gyms. Many people set up meditation or mindfulness corners or separate rooms in their homes. Many mindfulness practices involve quieting your mind of distractions and breathing in and out naturally, while focusing your attention on a phrase, a mantra, or a sensation, and then coming back to your breath. For decades, researchers have studied meditation's benefits for both physical, mental, and emotional health. My favorite practice is Sharon Salzberg's metta meditation, referred to several times in this book. Metta meditation always leaves me with a quieter inner self and a sweet and open feeling of loving-kindness toward others. I highly recommend it—there is no downside to spending time being still, noticing your feelings, and sending compassion to yourself and others!

Resources

Domestic and Emotional Abuse

These are organizations you can reach out to if you feel you need some help and guidance for yourself or others.

Crisis Text Line
www.crisistextline.org
Text: "HOME" to 741741

Day One
https://dayoneservices.org
Phone: 866-223-1111
Email: safety@dayoneservices.org

I'll Go First
www.illgofirst.com
Text: "GoFirst" to 741741

Jed Foundation
https://jedfoundation.org
Phone: 212-647-7544
Fax: 212-647-7542

Love Is Respect
www.loveisrespect.org
Phone: 866-331-9474; 866-331-8453 (TTY)
Text: "Loveis" to 22522

National Alliance on Mental Illness (NAMI)
https://nami.org
Phone: 800-950-6264
Text: 741741

National Coalition Against Domestic Violence (NCADV–State Coalitions)
ncadv.org/state-coalitions

National Domestic Violence Hotline
www.thehotline.org
Phone: 800-799-7233; 800-787-3224 (TTY)
Text: "START" to 88788

Safe Horizon
www.safehorizon.org
Phone: 800-621-4673

Women's Law Initiative
www.womenslaw.org
Phone: 800-799-7233; 800-787-3224 (TTY)

Women's Leadership

These groups offer an opportunity to meet and be inspired by like-minded individuals who focus unapologetically on celebrating and empowering women.

Fearlessly Girl
www.fearlesslygirl.com
This is an internationally recognized antibullying organization for girls.

Girls Leadership Institute
https://girlsleadership.org
Phone: 866-744-9102

Global Women's Leadership Network
https://cuwomen.org
Radically accelerate the empowerment of exceptional women through leadership development and an engaged global network.

Live Your Dream
www.liveyourdream.org
This movement is dedicated to ensuring every woman and girl has the opportunity to reach her full potential, be free from violence, and live her dreams.

National Organization for Women (NOW)
https://now.org
This organization is devoted to achieving full equality for women through education and litigation.

She Heroes
https://sheheroes.org
This organization empowers young girls of all backgrounds to dream big, explore their interests, and passionately pursue nontraditional careers.

Her Wisdom
www.herwisdom.org

Education, Empowerment, and Social and Emotional Learning

These organizations focus on providing a deeper understanding of the skills required to live a more meaningful and productive life and the opportunity to learn those skills.

Collaborative for Academic, Social, and Emotional Learning
https://casel.org
Phone: 312-226-3770
Fax: 312-226-3777

Consortium for Research on Emotional Intelligence in Organizations
https://www.eiconsortium.org

Star Factor Coaching
https://www.starfactorcoaching.com

The Empathy Effect
https://empathetics.com/the-empathy-effect

EmpathyWorks
https://empathyworks.org/about-us

Futures Without Violence
www.futureswithoutviolence.org

The New Pluralists
https://newpluralists.org

Greater Good Science Center
https://ggsc.berkeley.edu

Loss, Trauma, and Emotion Lab
www.tc.columbia.edu/LTElab

OJI Life Lab
https://ojilifelab.com

6 Seconds Emotional Intelligence Network
www.6seconds.org
Phone: 831-763-1800

Training Institute for Mental Health
www.timh.org
Phone: 212-627-8181
Fax: 646-638-3025

Village Counseling Center
https://villagecounselingcenter.net
Phone: 352-373-8189
Fax: 352-373-8190

Yale Center for Emotional Intelligence
https://ycei.org

The Moodsters
https://themoodsters.com

The Meeting House
https://www.themeetinghousesel.org

Individuals

These are people I have admired and whose work has been meaningful to me in my research, explorations, and in writing this book.

Angeles Arrien
www.angelesarrien.com

George Bonanno
https://georgebonanno.com

Richard Boyatzis
www.instituteofcoaching.org/richard-boyatzis

Marc Brackett
https://marcbrackett.com

Brené Brown
https://brenebrown.com

Susan Cain
https://susancain.net

Helen Churko
https://helenchurkocoaching.com

Diana Divecha
https://www.developmentalscience.com

Helen Fisher
https://helenfisher.com/

Daniel Goleman
www.danielgoleman.info

Adam Grant
http://www.adamgrant.net/

Jon Kabat-Zinn
https://www.mindfulnesscds.com

Courtney E. Marti
www.courtneyemartin.com

Sharon Salzberg
www.sharonsalzberg.com

Chris Scott
https://empathyworks.org/about us

Rachel Simmons
www.rachelsimmons.com

Sheila Ohlsson Walker
https://sheilaohlssonwalker.com

Niobe Way
https://steinhart.nyu.edu

Mind, Body, and Spirit

These groups inspire the practice of integrating the mental, physical, and spiritual aspect of our entire selves.

The Garrison Institute—Retreats
www.garrisoninstitute.org
Phone: 845-424-4800

International Taoist Tai Chi Society
https://taoist.org

The Joyful Heart Foundation
www.joyfulheartfoundation.org

National Women's Health Resource Center
www.healthywomen.org
Phone: 877-986-9472

Yoga Alliance
www.yogaalliance.org
Phone: 888-921-9642

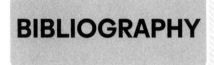
BIBLIOGRAPHY

River Story

Linklater, Kristin. 2006. *Freeing the Natural Voice,* revised edition. Los Angeles: Drama Publishers.

Sociogram

Moreno, Jacob Levy. 1934. *Who Shall Survive? A New Approach to the Problem of Human Interrelations.* New York: Beacon House.

Taking It Deeper

Brandchaft, B., S. Doctors, and D. Sorter. 2010. *Toward an Emancipatory Psychoanalysis: Brandchaft's Intersubjective Vision.* New York: Routledge.

Fonagy, P. 2001. *Attachment Theory and Psychoanalysis,* New York: Other Press.

Fosshage, J. L. 2005. "The Explicit and Implicit Domains in Psychoanalytic Change." In *Psychoanalytic Inquiry* 25, no. 4: 516–39.

Gallese, V. 2001. "The 'Shared Manifold' Hypothesis: From Mirror Neurons to Empathy." In *Journal of Consciousness Studies* 8, nos. 5–7: 33–50.

———. 2003a. "The Manifold Nature of Interpersonal Relations: The Quest for a Common Mechanism." *Philosophical Transactions of the Royal Society B* 358, no. 1431: 517–28.

———. 2003b. "The Roots of Empathy: The Shared Manifold Hypothesis and the Neural Basis of Intersubjectivity. *Psychopathology* 36, no. 4: 171–80.

———. 2005a. " 'Being Like Me': Self-Other Identity, Mirror Neuron, and Empathy." In *Perspectives on Imitation: From Cognitive Neuroscience to Social Science,* edited by S. Hurley and N. Chater, 1:101–18. Cambridge, MA: MIT Press.

———. 2005b. "Embodied Simulation: From Neurons to Phenomenal Experience." In *Phenomenology and the Cognitive Sciences* 4:23–48.

————. 2006. "Intentional Attunement: A Neurophysiological Perspective on Social Cognition and Its Disruption in Autism." In *Brain Research* 1079:15–24.

————. 2007. "Before and Below Theory of Mind: Embodied Simulation and the Neural Correlates of Social Cognition." In *Philosophical Transactions of the Royal Society B* 362, no. 1480: 659–69.

————. 2009. "Mirror Neurons, Embodied Simulation, and the Neural Basis of Social Identification." *Psychoanalytic Dialogues* 19:519–36.

————. 2010. "Embodied Simulation and Its Role in Intersubjectivity." In *The Embodied Self: Dimensions, Coherence, and Disorders,* edited by T. Fuchs, H. C. Sattel, and P. Henningsen. Stuttgart, Germany: Schattauer.

Gallese, V., L. Fadiga, L. Fogassi, and G. Rizzolatti. 1996. "Action Recognition in the Premotor Cortex." *Brain* 119, no. 2: 593–609.

Gallese, V., M. N. Eagle, and P. Migone. 2007. "Intentional Attunement: Mirror Neurons and the Neural Underpinnings of Interpersonal Relations." In *Journal of the American Psychoanalytic Association* 55:131–76.

Gallese, V., M. Rochat, G. Cossu, and C. Sinigaglia. 2009. "Motor Cognition and Its Role in the Phylogeny and Ontogeny of Intentional Understanding." In *Developmental Psychology* 45:103–13.

Gallese, V., and C. Sinigaglia. 2011. "What Is So Special About Embodied Simulation?" In *Trends in Cognitive Sciences* 15, no. 11: 512–19.

Gallese, V., M. A. Gernsbacher, C. Heyes, G. Hickok, and M. Iacoboni. 2011. "Mirror Neuron Forum." *Perspectives on Psychological Science* 6:369–404.

Gazzaniga, M. S. 2008. *Human: The Science Behind What Makes Us Unique.* New York: HarperCollins.

Hebb, D. O. 1949. *The Organization of Behavior: A Neuropsychological Theory.* New York: Wiley.

Kohut, H. 1959. "Introspection, Empathy, and Psychoanalysis." In *Journal of American Psychoanalytic Association* 7:459–83.

————. 1982. "Introspection, Empathy, and the Semi-Circle of Mental Health." In *International Journal of Psychoanalysis* 63:395–407.

————. 1984. *How Does Analysis Cure?* Chicago: University of Chicago Press.

Lachmann, F. M., and R. D. Stolorow. 1980. *Psychoanalysis of Developmental Arrests: Theory and Treatment.* Madison, CT: International Universities Press.

Lenoff, L. 1998, 2003. Published chapters in *Progress in Self Psychology,* Internet Editor of *The International Journal of Psychoanalytic Self Psychology.*

Livingston, M. 2001. *Vulnerable Moments: Deepening the Therapeutic Process.* New York: Jason Aronson.

————. 2015. "Interventions at an Impasse: Vulnerability, the Group Leader's Use of Self, and Sustained Empathic Focus as a Bridge between Theory and Practice." In *The One and the Many: Relational Approaches to Group Psychotherapy,* edited by R. Grossmark and F. Wright, 145–67. New York: Routledge.

Orange, D. M. 1995. *Emotional Understanding: Studies in Psychoanalytic Epistemology.* New York: Guilford Press.

Orange, D. M., G. E. Atwood, and R. D. Stolorow. 1997. *Working Intersubjectively: Contextualism in Psychoanalytic Practice.* Hillsdale, NJ: Analytic Press.

Scott, C. A. 2013. "Being Human Together: Empathy Revisited." Presentation given at the International Association for Psychoanalytic Self Psychology annual conference, Chicago.

————. 2016. "Deconstructing Empathy and Creating a 'We Space' in Group Therapy." *Group* 40, no. 2: 103.

Scott, C. A., and M. Livingston. 2017. "Sustained Empathic Focus and the Creation of a 'We Space' Revisited in Light of Recent Findings in Neurobiology." *International Journal of Group Psychotherapy* 67:479–99.

Stolorow, R. D. 1993. "Thoughts on the Nature and Therapeutic Action of Psychoanalytic Interpretation." In *The Widening Scope of Self Psychology: Progress in Self Psychology,* edited by A. Goldberg, 31–43. NY: Routledge.

Stolorow, R. D., G. E. Atwood, and B. Brandchaft. 1994. *The Intersubjective Perspective.* Northvale, NJ: Jason Aronson.

Winnicott, D. 1953. "Transitional Objects and Transitional Phenomena: A Study of the First Not-Me Possession." *International Journal of Psychoanalysis* 43:89–97.

———. *The Maturational Process and the Facilitating Environment: Studies in the Theory of Emotional Development.* Madison, CT: International Universities Press.

ACKNOWLEDGMENTS

I am deeply grateful to countless people who, through the years have shared their stories, engaged in conversations, and offered their wisdom and expertise. You have all contributed to my understanding and urgency to reach a general audience about how to spot gaslighting and psychological manipulation—and how to heal from it and thrive beyond it.

I feel so blessed to know my amazing literary agent, Richard Pine, who has believed not only in my message about gaslighting but also in the power of the human spirit to heal from its soul-destroying grip. You are an extraordinary model of what it means to care for and shine a light on other's ideas and wisdom—and for how healing happens when surrounded by lovingkindness. I am also grateful for Eliza Rothstein and her time, care, thoughtful attention, and support of my work on gaslighting these past years.

This book would not have happened without my wonderful team at Rodale: Diana Baroni, who said yes to the idea of a recovery guide for gaslighting; Michele Eniclerico, who worked with me and this manuscript insightfully, carefully, and consistently, and believed in the power of personal journey as an empowering learning experience and path to healing; and Elysia Liang, who guided me through the page layouts. Thanks to Odette Fleming, Tammy Blake, SallyAnne McCartin, Jacqui Daniels, and others who will support the book's launch!

Immense gratitude to my dear friend and advisor Helen Churko, who always listens to what is on my mind and in my heart, and what I am seeing in the world through the eyes of my patients. You are so gifted at helping light the next path (and the next one and the next one).

Great thanks to my dear friend and collaborator, Cynthia Dickason-Scott, whose incredible skills and originality transformed text into an interactive experience, and to Chris Scott, whose insight, extensive research, and work in self psychology and empathy was foundational for taking the psychological insights in this book deeper still. I am so grateful to you both.

My deep gratitude for the *The Gaslight Effect Podcast* team: Ryan Changcoco, Gabrielle Caoagas, Michael Lenz, and Salar Korangy. Thank you to Suzen Pettit and Marcus Estevev of Omaginarium for digital marketing. Thank you for believing in the power of my message, for your expertise and magic with growing audiences, and for the thoughtful design elements that bring knowledge about the Gaslight Effect to more people around the world.

Thank you to the many journalists and podcast hosts who have elevated gaslighting in the national and international conversation, most especially Maria Shriver, for hosting the *Today* show; Hara Marano and Kaja Perina at *Psychology Today,* for highlighting my blog; Jimmy Finkelstein, for introducing me to *Changing America* and *The Hill*—gratitude for the opportunity to publish my work and the work of Yale Center for Emotional Intelligence through the years; Katie Orenstein, founder of The OpEd Project, for ongoing learning about writing; Jen Muller, who has brilliantly edited my writing for years now; and to Vox Media, which published my article on gaslighting in 2019.

Since the publication of *The Gaslight Effect* in 2007 I have had many wonderful colleagues who have become lifelong friends. Gratitude to Dr. Laura Artusio, Andrea Portera, and Dafne for leading our work in Italy with heart and music; Dr. Diana Divecha, for our years of deep conversation and writing together about life, emotions, parenting, communication; Denise Daniels, for creating the Moodsters Family Foundation and opening the opportunity for a humanitarian mission for children of Ukraine; Leslee Udwin, for creating Think Equal; and Jamie Lockwood, for years of conversation, fun, and travel together.

I am profoundly grateful to everyone at the Yale Center for Emotional Intelligence, whose spirit, vision, and passion make working to change the world a joy every day. Most especially, our Center director, my colleague and dearest friend, Dr. Marc Brackett, and his family: Horacio Marquinez, Irene Crespi, Tutti, and Peque. And I so appreciate the opportunity to work closely with Michelle Lugo, Mariam Korangy, Danica Kelly, Nikki Elbertson,

Dr. Jennifer Allen, Dr. Zorana Pringle, Kathryn Lee, Dr. Christina Cipriano, Tangular Irby, Linda Torv, Zoe Sutters, Charlene Voyce, Jim Hagen, Dr. Craig Bailey, Dr. Jessica Hoffman, Julie McGarry, and all the fabulous Center staff and consultants. Deep gratitude to all of our advisors, most especially our Center champion and mentor, Charley Ellis, for years of sharing wisdom and to our former executive director, Scott Levy, for years of helping us move forward, and to Fran Rabinowitz, for sage counsel in matters of leadership.

Deep gratitude to all nurses and doctors at Yale New Haven Smilow Cancer Hospital and Yale New Haven Children's Hospital for the privilege of working with many of you over these last challenging years—your resilience and strength has been inspiring, especially the late Kathy Lyons, Dr. Roy Herbst, Marianne Hatfield, Lynn Sherman, Denine Baxter, and their leadership teams and staff.

Thank you to Cece Lipton, Hannah Husain, Hannah Herbst, and Krista Smith, the young women who have worked with me during the writing of this book, contributing original ideas to the science of emotional intelligence, and in bringing the message of gaslighting and psychological safety to the world.

Thank you to all my patients and students through the years—my profound gratitude for sharing your thoughts, feelings, dreams, and challenges with me. You are all courageous warriors in your own lives, and each of you have been my teachers, too.

Surprising and meaningful projects about gaslighting, healing, and resilience have come my way through colleagues and friends thinking deeply about how to use the arts to highlight the devastating effect of gaslighting and the power to heal. Thank you to Alan Maraynas, who is writing a movie script right now! Thank you TUCKER for the joy of providing a voiceover about my work and working with you on "Can't Help Myself."

There are so many people—friends and colleagues—who have been part of my inner circle in the last years and with whom I have had particularly meaningful conversations about gaslighting, emotionally abusive relationships, and recovery: I share my profound gratitude to Barbara Winston, Stephanie Wolkoff Winston, Pamela Gross, Dr. Heidi Brooks, Dr. George Bonnano, Kenny Becker, Ellyn Solis, Robin Bernstein, Dr. Janet Patti, Linda Lantieri, Wende Jager Hyman, Tara Bracco, Jolie Roberts, Andy Faas, Katharine Rupe, Dr. Debra Rozenzweig, Dr. Tripp Evans, Les Lenoff, Claire Aidem, Michele Savitz, Julie Appel, Jessica Baxter, Dr. Alice Forester, Dr. Niobe Way, Dr. Sheila Ohlssohn, Walker, Lynn Kressel, Shelley Gliedman, Rosana Butler, Katie Embree, and Susan Collins. Thanks especially to Joan Finkelstein for endless conversations about the road to healing.

My acknowledgments would not be complete without expressing my profound gratitude for the people who have cared for my children and enriched my life in many ways for many years. First and foremost: Lena Gordon and Lisa Neal and family—deepest love and thank-yous; Enrique and Carmen Michel; Dr. Larry Hirsch, Dr. Yemi Damisah, and the physicians in neurology and medicine at Yale New Haven Hospital; our longtime family physician, Dr. Bertie Bregman, and all of Westside Family Medicine; Damian Paglia and Liz Torres; Doug George; Chris Bermudez; Dorota Bovee and Claudia Vasquez; and Brandon McHie.

I would not be so blessed as to offer this book to the world, were it not for my wonderful parents: Roz and Dave Stern, who loved me always, nurtured me, pushed me, and supported me. They would be so happy to know that so many people have been helped by reading my books.

I share my heartfelt gratitude, always, to my cherished and fun-filled family: Eric, Jacquie, Justin, Chelsea, Sofia, Saige, Daniel, Julia, Charlie, Lainey, Jan, Billy, Max, Marcia, Larry, Nancy, Bob, Doug, Shari, Kate, Jonah, Jessie, and Pepper. I am so lucky to have you all in my life.

To my wonderful husband, Mel, who believes in the power to choose the life you want to live and the healing power of my work. So much love and a million thank-yous for your ongoing support of my work.

And deepest gratitude most especially to my truly awesome children, Scott and Melissa, who light up my life every day and whose commitment to making a difference in the world fills my heart with pride and joy. I am so heartened you will know how fulfilling Tikkun Olam can be.

INDEX

ABOUT THE AUTHOR

Robin Stern, PhD, is the cofounder and associate director of the Yale Center for Emotional Intelligence and co-developer of RULER, an evidence-based approach adopted by over 4,000 schools worldwide. She is a licensed psychoanalyst with thirty years of experience and the author of *The Gaslight Effect* and *Project Rebirth*. She serves on several advisory boards, including the International Society for Emotional Intelligence, Crisis Text Line, HerWisdom, I'll Go First, and Think Equal. Dr. Stern regularly consults with schools and companies around the world and is cofounder of Star Factor Leadership Coaching and of Oji Life Lab, an innovative digital learning system for emotional intelligence.